ICONIC HOTELS AND MOTELS *of* CAPE COD

Christopher Setterlund

Published by The History Press
Charleston, SC
www.historypress.com

First published 2021

Manufactured in the United States

ISBN 9781467144094

Library of Congress Control Number: 2021931122

Notice: The information in this book is true and complete to the best of our knowledge. It is offered without guarantee on the part of the author or The History Press. The author and The History Press disclaim all liability in connection with the use of this book.

This book is dedicated with love to my nieces and nephews. Kaleigh, Emma, Liam, Landon, Lucas and Sylvie, thank you for bringing joy to my life and making growing older not seem so bad.

CONTENTS

Contents

ACKNOWLEDGEMENTS

This project would not have been possible without the love and support of my very large extended family. In addition to those whom the book is dedicated to, I wish to thank my mother, Laurie; my sisters, Katie, Lindsay and Ashley; my brother, Matt; my Nina Rosemarie Sullivan; my Grampa John Sullivan and Nana Doris Setterlund, both in heaven; my father, Jack; my aunts, Kelly, Susan, Emma and Amy; my uncles, Bob, Steve, Eric and John; my cousins, Patrick, Sarah, Keith, Ryane, Tracey and Kathleen; and the people who are so close to me that they have been like family for ages: Serpa, Brenda, Grace, Debbie and the entire Clark family, Maui, Deanna and Mike.

I'd like to thank the crew of amazing friends who have supported this journey from the start, more recently or even before my writing adventure began. Thank you to Steve and Amanda; Monique; D.J.W.; Shayna; Dawn; Barry; John Z.; Greg; Mike G.; my old Marsh crew, Meg, Judy, Barbara, Brian, Mason, Timmy, Kristin and Dana; my Mayflower gang, Barbie, Carol, Keith, Krista, Kelly, Stephanie, Deb, Marina and Janson; Fitzy and Cape Cloth; Emily Wood; Meghan and the Jones family; Katie and the Bunker family; and the great Bill DeSousa-Mauk. Without them, this book would not exist

Thank you to all who helped me with the research and information gathering for this project, including the wonderful people and resources at the Sturgis Library, Kara Lachance and the amazing people at Wequassett, Bob Higgins and the great people at New Seabury/Popponesset, Barbara

A postcard of the Belmont Hotel. *Courtesy of the Boston Public Library.*

Stone Amidon of the Lighthouse Inn, Falmouth Public Library, Elizabeth Stefan of Ocean Edge, Don Broderick and the Atwood House Museum of Chatham, Lauren Niegos and Chatham Bars Inn, Carol Saunders and the Hyannis Public Library.

INTRODUCTION

Since the latter half of the nineteenth century, Cape Cod has been a popular vacation destination. From horses and buggies to electric automobiles, and from telegraph to email, times and technology have changed. Yet one thing remains the same, the people come in droves. Beaches, shops, restaurants, history and culture—these are a few of the things that bring people back. When on the Cape, individuals and families need a place to stay; that is where the places on the following pages come in. From the small and quaint bed-and-breakfasts to five-star world-renowned resorts, there are some that have been lost to the annals of time and others that still beckon weary travelers to this day. These are some of the iconic hotels and resorts of Cape Cod.

ABERDEEN HALL

ADDRESS: GREAT ISLAND ROAD, WEST YARMOUTH
YEARS ACTIVE: 1902–1924

Great Island in West Yarmouth is perhaps the most restricted location on all of Cape Cod. There are no less than three layers of security standing between the guarded entrance to the elite neighborhood and the tip where Point Gammon Lighthouse stands. For nearly a century, this has been the case, as the posh homes that dot the eight-hundred-acre land mass are owned and visited by the cream of the crop of society. Few people realize that it was once public property.

Initially, it was home to only a smallpox hospital at the turn of the nineteenth century; a lighthouse was later added to aid navigation. These were the only inhabitants of the massive Great Island for the vast majority of the 1800s. It began to change in 1883, when ornithologist Charles Cory inherited his family's fortune and purchased the entire property from Samuel Payson for use as a game preserve as well as his summer home. Though he would occasionally open up his property for events such as concerts, Cory kept it private, much as it is today. After developing an affinity for golf in 1897, Cory had a private course built on Great Island. This led to the creation of Cory's own high-class country club, which was frequented by America's elite. It was called Aberdeen Hall.

Cory and Henry Fick built the club in 1902 at a cost of $100,000 ($3 million in 2021). The forty-five-bedroom structure was frequented by fellow elite members of society by invite only. There were numerous invitational golf tournaments held on the property, which made great use of Aberdeen Hall. After only a few years, however, Cory leased his country club to E.M.

Guild, the manager of the successful Sea Cliff Inn on Nantucket, for use as a first-class hotel in 1905.

The new use of Aberdeen Hall was an immediate success, with countless locals registering for a stay at the hotel. In January 1909, Cory sold the entirety of Great Island at auction due to heavy losses in the stock market. The eight-hundred-acre property, Aberdeen Hall, the golf links, a cottage, a water tower, a stable and a barn were purchased by New York steel magnate Henry Phipps. He immediately got to work, improving Aberdeen Hall and heavily promoting it as the "only first-class hotel on Cape." Phipps built a large addition in May 1909, and he brought in A.W. MacDougall to manage the property.

During the summer of 1909, Aberdeen Hall was full beyond capacity as locals and visitors flocked to Great Island. Offering private baths, fine dining, fishing, walks in the pine and oak tree groves, as well as rounds on the golf links, it was no wonder that Aberdeen Hall was the place to be. For those who were not able to make it to the hotel via automobile or on foot, a ferry service was put into place to shuttle people to the property from the Ocean Street Docks in Hyannis.

Before the hotel reopened for the 1911 season, Phipps paid the United States Dredging and Irrigation Company of New York to come to Great Island. The company's job was to drain the bogs and marsh lands on the property in an effort to rid the area of mosquitoes, which had become a black cloud over the otherwise terrific vacation spot. It is unknown if the efforts were successful.

Aberdeen Hall saw continued success, even after a change in management to Frances Yeager in 1912 ended in her declaring bankruptcy two years later. It was around this time, in 1914, that Rhode Island banker Malcolm Chace purchased Great Island. He kept Aberdeen Hall running smoothly and installed George Heely as manager. The hotel saw its greatest heights in terms of occupancy, including its most successful season, in 1919, after Chace's purchase.

The reign of Aberdeen Hall sadly ended on August 3, 1924, when a fire burned it to the ground. The fire began in an old laundry room, spread to the water tower and, finally, to the hotel. It took nearly forty-five minutes for the fire to reach the hotel, meaning that if it had been noticed earlier, perhaps the iconic building could have been saved. Luckily, all of the staff, as well as the fifty-eight guests who were staying there at the time, made it out safely. Firefighters came from as far away as Falmouth and Orleans, but the fire was a total loss, causing $200,000 in damage ($3.06 million in 2021).

With Aberdeen Hall gone, the time of Great Island being open to the public ended as well. Today, the vast majority of the property is still owned by the Chace family, with security patrolling year-round and home values averaging in several millions of dollars. The island and its homes are private, and the property should be respected. The only true way to catch glimpses of Great Island is via boat or being lucky enough to know someone with a home out there.

BARNSTABLE INN/GLOBE HOTEL

ADDRESS: 300 MAIN STREET, BARNSTABLE
YEARS ACTIVE: 1827–1972

Over the last several decades, Cape Cod has changed and modernized exponentially. Some places have maintained their classic charm, despite being firmly entrenched in the twenty-first century. Although Barnstable Village, along Route 6A remains one of the quaintest spots on the Cape, a huge part of its history is no longer there. The Barnstable Inn reigned supreme for more than a century across the street from the Barnstable District Court. The roots of this icon began all the way back in the eighteenth century.

The property that would become the Barnstable Inn first saw life in 1639. On this property, a family home was built for Reverend John Lothrop after his arrival from England. Many decades later, in 1799, a home was built for Anne Eldridge and her family. This was the beginning of a legend. The home remained just like any other for nearly thirty years, until Anna's sons Waterman and Eben had an idea. In 1827, the Barnstable District Courthouse was being finished up, and the young Eldridge brothers thought it would be a smart move to turn their two-story home into a hotel. The new seasonal hotel, situated on twelve acres of land on Main Street in Barnstable Village, would be called the Globe Hotel.

The Eldridge brothers set out to make their new hotel a hit for weary travelers, and they succeeded. It was seen as a place for solo travelers and those with families. At times during its first few decades, the Globe Hotel and the surrounding village were seen as being almost too quiet and relaxing. The Globe Hotel was immensely popular, as it was only a twelve-mile stagecoach ride from the end of the railroad in Sandwich and had a large stable and bowling alley. The sprawling land was dotted with fruit trees, with five elms shading the property along the street. Stagecoaches arrived and departed several times daily, and those who came to stay, usually for weeks at a time, were centrally located near many of the Cape attractions of the time. Icons of history stayed there, like Abraham Lincoln and Daniel Webster. The northwest bedroom became known as the Judge's Room, as it had the distinction of sheltering perhaps more lawyers than any other room in the country. Orange-and-yellow-tinged hard pine floors welcomed the visitors inside.

Waterman and Eben were front and center at the inn for more than two decades. Then they decided to take a risk on the California gold rush in 1850 and leased out their hotel to Seth Bartlett. He kept the positive reputation of the hotel going during his tenure; however, it was tragically short-lived. In early March 1852, Bartlett fell from a stagecoach and died a few weeks later. Waterman and Eben Eldridge had not succeeded out west and stepped back in as the faces of the establishment mere days later. The brothers remained in charge of the Globe Hotel until the early 1870s, when it was passed down to James Eldridge, Eben's son, after their deaths.

The Globe Hotel endured its biggest change in April 1897, when Susan B. Bangs took over the property. After moving to the Cape with her husband, Dr. E.M. Bangs from St. Paul, Minnesota, Bangs changed the name of the hotel to the Barnstable Inn. The rates for the hotel remained reasonable considering it was such an icon. Rooms cost $2.50 per day ($78.79 in 2021), with meals costing $0.50 for breakfast and lunch and $0.75 for dinner ($15.76 and $23.64 in 2021, respectively).

Bangs only stayed at the hotel until 1902, when she received an offer she couldn't refuse as the superintendent of the Franklin Square House, a home for working women in Boston. Although Bangs left for Boston, the name she gave the former Globe Hotel remained. The property stayed in the Eldridge family, with others serving as its manager in the early twentieth century, including Allen Nickerson, who spent fifteen years as the manager. The hotel was consistently updated inside, but it kept up its old-time charm on the outside.

James Eldridge, who had long since moved away from Cape Cod, finally sold the venerable hotel to the then-current manager Joseph Turpin in September 1924. After nearly a century and thousands of satisfied guests, this was the first time the property had not belonged to the Eldridge family since its inception.

The Barnstable Inn was in good hands under Turpin. In his time as manager, he had already improved the property; he had installed curbing and added a trellis on the back of the west side of the building. As the owner, his dedication to the hotel continued. The rooms were all renovated and redecorated in time for the 1926 season, and the building was repainted for the 1928 season. The building was later enlarged to include four stories. A pair of cottages were also added, and by the time Turpin sold the hotel it could house forty to fifty guests. He sold the Barnstable Inn in March 1946 to Lewis Bornstein of Brookline.

In the years following World War II, the hotel continued to flourish before eventually being sold to Walter Oldfield in the mid-1950s. It wasn't until after Oldfield sold the hotel to the Elmwood Corporation in October 1964 that the story began to change. In May 1965, a fire broke out due to faulty basement wiring, and although it was quickly extinguished by the Barnstable Fire Department, it was a sign of things to come. Massive renovations were planned once Barnstable Inn was purchased by Massachusetts senator Allen F. Jones in February 1967. These renovations included the addition of an eighty-four-by-sixty-two-foot building that contained twenty-four bedroom units and dining facilities. Despite questions about sewage and the potential for the drastically larger building to spoil the quaint Barnstable Village, the plans were approved in February 1968. However, the plans fell into litigation with wary locals, and Jones stated that the hotel was operating at a loss. It seemed Barnstable Inn was on borrowed time.

The iconic hotel continued unchanged in the 1969 season, but the renovations were overwhelming, as the building was falling into disrepair. The hotel's last gasp came in January 1971, when Leonard Healy of the Velvet Hammer nightclub bought the property. Healy had several in-depth surveys done to see whether or not the inn could be salvaged. It was reported that fixing the plumbing and heating alone would cost $125,000 ($807,000 in 2021). Dejected, Healy gave up the fight, and the oldest continuously operated hotel on Cape Cod was set to be razed.

Before it could be demolished, another fire nearly destroyed the property in November 1971. Ultimately, it fell victim to the wrecking ball in January 1972, making the property empty for the first time since 1799. Although Healy initially planned to rebuild the hotel, it never happened. Years later, the property saw new life with the arrival of Barnstable Tavern and Restaurant, along with office and retail space. In 2019, Barnstable Tuscan Cuisine opened on the property and was still in operation as of 2020.

THE CAPE CODDER

ADDRESS: CAPE CODDER ROAD, FALMOUTH
YEARS ACTIVE: 1900–1988

It began as a sheep farm overlooking Buzzards Bay. In the twenty-first century, it became occupied by luxury condominiums. During the time in between, however, it was considered one of the most beloved hotels on Cape Cod. Nestled in the village of Sippewissett in Falmouth is the story of the Cape Codder.

In the mid- to late nineteenth century, the property that would one day be home to a luxury waterfront resort for travelers was occupied by different guests: sheep. The property, which was owned by Richard L. Swift and then his heirs, was a 180-acre sheep farm in Falmouth's village of Sippewissett. It was prime real estate facing Buzzards Bay on Cape Cod's west coast, and Swift's heirs knew it. In 1892, the entire property was sold to Boston music producer John C. Haynes for $10,000 ($287,400 in 2021). Haynes divided much of the land up into lots for homes, while a large chunk, located at Hamblin Point, was saved for his pet project, a summer resort hotel on the water.

It would take several years before work began on the hotel. In the meantime, Haynes hired contractors to work on the land and roads that made up the property. In 1899, construction began on his dream hotel, which would be called Sippewissett Hotel. Its grand opening occurred on June 17, 1900. Haynes spared no expense, as the hotel had all of the best accommodations of the day. Costing a total of nearly $160,000 ($5 million in 2021), the Sippewissett had a golf course, a pier, a horse stable, bath houses, tennis courts, bowling alleys and a casino for dances. Its amenities and location made the hotel an immediate success. In its second season, in 1901, it was routinely filled to a capacity with more than 60 guests. The popularity of his new hotel made Haynes think about expansion. In 1902, the Sippewissett Hotel added fifty rooms, a large office, a thirty-four-by-eighty-foot dining room and a piazza that wrapped around the entirety of the hotel, nearly one-eighth of a mile. The enlarged four-story hotel debuted for the 1902 season with an increased capacity of 250.

The Colonial Revival style of the hotel perfectly complemented the tremendous sea breezes and sunsets of Buzzards Bay. John C. Haynes had created a destination for summer vacationers; however, he would not get to enjoy it for very long. Haynes died in May 1907 at the age of seventy-seven. After his death, the hotel came under the ownership of Joseph Meader and Albert Geiger Jr., who promptly changed its name to Hotel Cleveland. After one season, in July 1908, the pair sold the hotel to Percival F. Brine, who changed its name back to the Sippewissett Hotel for the 1909 season.

The hotel was sold in 1912, when Brine left to run the Pilgrim House hotel in Plymouth. The Sippewissett Club Inc. group bought the property in 1917 and called it the Sippewissett Club. It was called a "high-class motor club house," and it was run by Francis Howe for a few seasons until it was sold again in April 1919. This marked the fourth time in ten years that the hotel's name had been changed, as it then became known as Falmouth Arms. Despite its views, luxurious rooms and modern amenities, the hotel was seemingly in a constant state of instability. This continued in the spring of 1927, when the Falmouth Arms was bought by Charles Dooley and renamed the Mayflower Hotel, after a series of properties he owned in Hyannis, Osterville and Plymouth. Much like all of the hotel's previous owners, with the exception of Percival Brine, Dooley operated it at a loss.

Percival F. Brine once again owned the hotel in April 1931. He purchased it after Dooley lost it to bankruptcy and renamed it the Cape Codder. Brine paired the name change with extensive remodeling of the property, as he hoped to restore the luster it had when he originally owned it. The first two seasons were a success; however, the Great Depression began to take its toll, and in March 1933, foreclosure proceedings began. Despite delays, as the locals tried to help Brine maintain his hotel, he lost ownership of the Cape Codder in 1936.

Melton Waters opened the hotel for the 1936 season, and he procured a liquor license for the new restaurant inside the hotel, the Fisherman's Grill. The restaurant was decorated with nautical themes, red drapes and sea green walls. Waters insisted on pristine manicured landscaping around the hotel and had the exterior of the building repainted. In July 1936, a pair of slot machines were seized from the hotel by Falmouth Police. Although it was seen as a minor infraction, Waters was no longer the manager shortly thereafter. John and Shirley Peterson then took over the hotel's ownership, and the Cape Codder finally got the stability it sorely needed.

For the grand reopening of the Fisherman's Grill and the hotel in general, in June 1937, there was a big celebration, which included former heavyweight boxing champion Jack Dempsey. The new owners had buses meet arriving trains for guests. In 1946, the Petersons had a 125-by-35-foot outdoor swimming pool built at a cost of $100,000 ($1.34 million in 2021). In 1943, Peterson also took over ownership of the Park Beach Hotel in Falmouth Heights, giving him properties on either side of the town.

By the late 1940s, the Cape Codder was the largest hotel under one roof on Cape Cod. It included a fifty-four-room annex and a new kitchen that was capable of serving 1,500 people a night. Peterson sought to be all-inclusive when it came to guests at his resort, as he chose to charge modest rates; this allowed more than just the rich to come and stay at the hotel. In 1949, Peterson purchased one of the oldest farms on Cape Cod. Originally owned by John Weeks in 1679, it had been run by the Weeks family for generations. Peterson used this farm to grow the crops that were used at his Cape Codder

Cape Codder Club Condos in Falmouth. *Courtesy of Christopher Setterlund.*

Hotel. Peterson also pushed for the construction of breakwaters to protect the beaches near the hotel. He recognized, even in the 1940s and 1950s, that the coastline was precious and a huge contributing factor to vacationers choosing Cape Cod. Stability and prosperity finally came for the Cape Codder and the Petersons throughout their tenure as the owners.

In 1980, after more than four decades in charge, the Petersons sold the Cape Codder to the Boston-based chain Hotels of Distinction for $1.5 million ($4.76 million in 2021). The group held on to the iconic property for five years before selling it to International Developers Inc. John Peterson, the Cape Codder's longtime owner, died in 1986, before the final bell came for the property. In 1988, the hotel was razed in order to make room for the condominium complex Cape Codder Club, which was opened in 1999 and still stood as of 2020. The Peterson farm property near Woods Hole Road was bought by the town of Falmouth in 1998; it has since been converted to conservation land.

CHATHAM BARS INN

ADDRESS: 297 SHORE ROAD, CHATHAM
YEARS ACTIVE: 1914–PRESENT

For more than a century, Chatham Bars Inn has combined luxurious amenities with breathtaking views. It is no wonder that it has been consistently successful since its inception in the years before World War I.

Chatham Bars Inn was the brainchild of Charles Ashley Hardy, who lived in Wayland, Massachusetts, but had ancestors from Chatham. He chose land that had formerly been owned by his descendants in the prominent Sears family as the location for his luxury resort. The site was located on a hill along Shore Road, which overlooked Aunt Lydia's Cove, North Beach and the Atlantic Ocean. In the spring of 1914, with the hotel nearing completion, the furniture trucks that were coming from Boston became newsworthy events, as they passed through each Cape town along the way. On Tuesday, June 9, 1914, Hardy invited the entire town of Chatham to come and inspect his creation. It was a dry run for the opening night festivities, which occurred the following day, June 10.

The hotel's opening night was a tremendous success. It included music from Fogg's Orchestra of Brockton, along with cake, ice cream and nearly all of Chatham, with people from all of the towns in Cape Cod in attendance. The new three-story luxury resort boasted swimming at a private beach, tennis courts, a small farm and a golf course, among other amenities. On entering, guests would encounter a spacious lobby; the south lounge was dotted with wicker furniture, and the fifty-seven-by-seventy-eight-foot dining area could seat more than two hundred people at a time.

The view of the ocean from the front steps of Chatham Bars Inn. *Courtesy of Christopher Setterlund.*

Hardy desired to make Chatham Bars Inn totally self-sufficient, meaning guests could come and stay and have everything they could possibly need right there on the grounds. One of the first big-name guests at the new resort was Cape Cod author Joseph Lincoln. Shortly after opening, a pier was constructed, which allowed guests to walk across the cove to North Beach. Initially, the resort was seasonal, opening in May and closing just after Columbus Day, which reflected the very quiet off-season of Cape Cod.

In February 1916, a large fire, which burned the home of Postmaster Nathaniel Eldridge, nearly made it to Chatham Bars Inn; however, it was stopped before reaching the resort and its ten cottages. The entire property was valued at $200,000 ($4.8 million in 2021) at that time. Chatham was beginning to boom as a summer resort town and tourist attraction, partially thanks to Hardy's beautiful hotel.

Hardy oversaw Chatham Bars Inn as a respite for the societal elite, many of whom enjoyed hunting. He arranged trips all over Chatham and out onto

Monomoy Island for his guests. In a sad bit of irony, a solo hunting trip spelled the end for Charles Ashley Hardy. On December 1, 1929, Hardy's body was found a few hundred yards from Mill Pond, near his own cottage. He had died from an accidental shotgun blast at the age of fifty-five. The creator of Chatham Bars Inn and its owner of fifteen years left behind an impressive legacy, and it was a mantle others were willing to pick up.

In the aftermath of Hardy's loss, his luxury resort was taken over by Chatham Associates, a land trust group Hardy had formed in the years before his death. The property was bought from the group on January 1, 1953, by Edwin McMullen, a commercial real estate associate who had summered in Chatham for years. Although the exterior structure of Chatham Bars Inn was not changed, McMullen made several interior improvements. These changes included installing showers and correcting the electricity, which would habitually turn off at 7:00 p.m. Under McMullen's watch, the resort hosted such luminaries as William Rockefeller, Henry Ford and the royal family of Holland. During the 1970s and into the early 1980s, the kitchen served an average of 1,300 to 1,400 meals a day, and up to 140 people staffed the kitchen during the peak summer months. McMullen also promoted the early spring and late fall "shoulder" seasons to help keep the inn busy longer.

McMullen oversaw the eighty-acre resort for more than thirty years before finally selling the property in late 1986 for $23 million ($54.9 million in 2021) to Alan Green and William Langelier. The new owners were the first to keep Chatham Bars Inn opened year round. Although this was an important change in the day-to-day operation of the hotel, it was the only major change Green and Langelier enacted, as their run was brief. They sold the resort in 1993 to the Great American Insurance Co. of Cincinnati. The property was sold again in 2006 to Richard Cohen of Capital Properties. Cohen spent $100 million on renovations, redoing every room of the property and every cottage, but he maintained the hotel's original charm.

Chatham Bars Inn has overlooked the Atlantic Ocean for more than a century, and there are no signs of it slowing down. It is known worldwide as a world-class resort, and its 217 rooms and suites are routinely filled with travelers from all over the globe. The inn hosts many special events, like weddings, and its four public restaurants continue to be supplied with produce from the eight-acre Chatham Bars Inn Farm. What started as a semi-private playground for the powerful elite has continued to grow and evolve over the decades into a Cape Cod landmark. The hotel's commitment to its guests has not changed since day one.

CHATHAM INN AT 359 MAIN STREET/CRANBERRY INN

ADDRESS: 359 MAIN STREET, CHATHAM
YEARS ACTIVE: 1884–PRESENT

Through name changes and renovations, this spot is proof that an establishment can improve and evolve with the times. Nestled along the quaint yet bustling Main Street of Chatham, Chatham Inn is constantly adding to its laundry list of awards and achievements, including being Cape Cod's only Relais & Châteaux hotel. It is surrounded by the beauty of Cape Cod outside, and it surrounds its guests with luxury inside. The Chatham Inn got its start more than a century ago, when it had a different name and when Cape Cod was truly a different place.

Long before Wi-Fi, television, radio, paved roads and even electricity, the property that one day became known as the Chatham Inn was gaining traction. It first saw the light of day in 1830, when Gideon and Reliance Small, fresh off the boat from England, built their home on present-day Main Street. It remained a family home for decades. After Gideon died in 1861, Reliance sold the home to their sea captain son Sylvester. He, too, used it as a family home until 1884, when he began opening it to tourists. Captain Small gave the property the name Traveler's Home.

The venture was an immediate success for Small, and he found himself having to enlarge the building during the summer of 1885, changing it to look more like a resort than a family home. Small's hotel was enlarged to twenty rooms, and it included a shed big enough for ten horses and a private well compactly located on one acre of land. Those changes were also a success, and 1886 was a booming year for business, according to the

The Chatham Inn at 359 Main Street. *Courtesy of Christopher Setterlund.*

local newspaper. Traveler's Home became the seasonal headquarters for the Norfolk Hunting Club, which would arrive via railroad with its horses and dogs to throngs of giddy onlookers.

In May 1891, Small's wife, Derinda, died suddenly, and Sylvester rapidly lost interest in running the hotel. By the summer of 1893, he had put the Traveler's Home up for sale. The high-class guests who patronized the hotel were a big selling point for the next owners, as the property was sold at auction on July 9, 1894, to Captain Joshua Nickerson and a group of others. Small left Chatham for New Hampshire shortly thereafter. The new ownership only lasted until 1898, when John Farmer bought the hotel and renamed it Monomoyick Inn, after the tribe of Natives who once inhabited the Lower Cape.

Farmer immediately took to repainting and renovating the property to make it his own, and this only increased the legacy of the business that was begun by Captain Small. Farmer and his wife, Mary, entertained a routinely full house throughout the summer months for twenty years. After John Farmer's death in December 1918, Mary continued to run Monomoyick on her own. She sold the property to Carl and Doris Chandler, experienced hotel folk from Quincy, before the 1935 season. Mary passed away the following year at the age of eighty-three.

The Chandlers made one big change to the Monomoyick Inn: they added food service to the hotel in the form of the Flying Cloud Breakfast Room. Stability and prosperity followed for the Chandlers and the Monomoyick Inn throughout the remainder of the 1930s and into the 1940s. Changes came fast in the 1950s. It all began with the Chandlers selling Monomoyick to George Noyes in 1953. Noyes's big contribution to the history of the property was a name change. The Monomoyick Inn became the Cranberry Inn shortly after his purchase, and it was then repainted cranberry red. Noyes's tenure as owner was short-lived, and he sold the hotel to the McGaw family in 1955. The McGaws ran the inn and restaurant until 1963, when they sold it to Mary and Richard Hamilton for $6,000 ($51,200 in 2021).

Both of the Hamiltons had previous connections to the property. Richard's mother had worked there when it was the Traveler's Home in 1886, and Mary herself had worked there as a server in 1929, when it was the Monomoyick. Their connection helped add to the iconic property's legacy. Soon, Mary was fully in charge, and she put more emphasis on the fifty-seat restaurant of the Cranberry Inn; this included serving 240 people for breakfast in the two small dining rooms one Fourth of July. From blueberry pancakes and cranberry muffins to Yankee pot roast and cocktails, Mary Hamilton thrilled customers with the food while charming them with the old inn atmosphere. Prior to the 1981 season, Hamilton sold the inn to John Droney, as she went on to become a trustee at the Eldredge Library. The Droney family added their own flare to the historic property, including a new name: the Cranberry Inn at Chatham. They held on to the business until October 1988, when it was sold to Richard Morris and Peg DeHan.

Morris and DeHan closed the inn for extensive renovations with an eye on a grand reopening. Private bathrooms were added to each of the fourteen rooms on the east side of the building. All of the floors were refinished, and the new owners got a full liquor license to serve in Schooners Tavern Taproom, which overlooked Main Street. In June 1989, the Cranberry Inn reopened to much success and fanfare. Morris and DeHan sold it in 1994 to Jim and Debbie Bradley, who carried out more renovations on the property. The property changed hands again and was eventually owned by Paul and Lauri Benk in 2013.

In the 2010s, the Cranberry Inn evolved from an iconic historic inn to one of the premier hotels in the United States. The Benks changed the hotel's name to Chatham Inn at 359 Main, and after it was purchased by Jeff and Kayla Ippoliti, a four-year remodeling project took place and was completed in 2019. Today, the eighteen-room boutique hotel claims numerous accolades, including being the only four-star boutique hotel on Cape Cod. The Chatham Wine Bar inside the hotel is considered one of the best restaurants on the Cape, and it is a AAA four-diamond hotel.

From its humble beginnings as the Small family home, to its legacy building days as the Cranberry Inn and all the way up to its current iteration as a high-class luxury hotel, the property at 359 Main Street has seen changes in Chatham and has evolved with them.

CHATHAM WAYSIDE INN

ADDRESS: 512 MAIN STREET, CHATHAM
YEARS ACTIVE: 1914–PRESENT

Charming and historic in a town that defines "charming and historic," the Wayside Inn of Chatham has been greeting countless guests and diners for more than 150 years. Throughout its existence on quaint Main Street, whether as a sea captain's home, a stagecoach stop, a high-class restaurant or an award-winning hotel, this icon has remained a destination in Chatham.

The property at 512 Main Street first saw development in 1859, when it became the home of Captain Joseph Nickerson and his wife, Mary. On June 10, 1862, the home was opened as a hotel for the first time, and it was called the Nauset House. Even in its early form, it was seen as having first-class accommodations, along with a prime location and a popular landlord in Nickerson. The Nauset House was visited by hundreds of people in its first week and was referred to, at the time, as the centerpiece that tied the village of Chatham together.

Nickerson closed the Nauset House the following year to the disappointment of many. It remained a private residence until it was purchased in 1867 by Isaiah Harding, who reopened it as a hotel for the summer season. Nickerson moved to Boothbay, Maine, after selling his house. The property saw an immediate crush of success, just as it had when it initially opened. However, Harding did not choose to hold on to it for very long, and it was put up for sale in 1871. It sat on the market for more than a year before it was bought by Charles H. Smith in December 1872. Smith resigned his post as assistant keeper of the twin Chatham Lighthouses to take on the property. He ran it

Chatham Wayside Inn. *Courtesy of Christopher Setterlund.*

successfully until he got the urge to return to the lighthouses, and he sold the Nauset House at auction on December 20, 1879. Levi Eldridge became the hotel's new owner and sold it almost immediately to W.R. Taylor the following summer. Despite its reputation as a first-class hotel, the Nauset House had been sold five times in less than twenty years. Taylor changed its name to the Ocean House and kept it open for a few years. However, in April 1884, Taylor decided to retire from the hotel business, closing the Ocean House and making it a private home again.

In April 1893, Captain William H. Berry retired from his three-masted schooner, the *John S. Davis*, after purchasing the home. Berry opened the Ocean House again, much to the delight of the people of Chatham. He spent months getting it ready for a grand June reopening, even traveling across the country to find a suitable chef for the property. It was an immediate success yet again, thanks, in large part, to the warm and congenial nature of Berry. But tragedy struck for the owner in June 1895, when his wife, Rosa, died suddenly at the age of forty. He could have let his loss take his business down, but he doubled down and enlarged the Ocean House to better serve more travelers in the spring of 1897. In 1898, after only five years of running the property, Berry was in charge of the dominant hotel in Chatham; it was a year-round destination and was referred to as "old reliable."

Once again, as it was becoming an established high-class hotel, change came. In May 1901, the Ocean House was closed and was turned back into a private residence. It remained as such for more than a decade before Frank R. Taylor purchased it in 1914. Taylor made mass changes, bringing in all new furnishings, changing it back to a hotel and adding an ice cream parlor. On May 15, 1914, Taylor held the grand opening of his hotel, the Wayside Inn.

Taylor changed the hotel to a seasonal destination on its opening, and he highlighted the property's horse stables to prospective visitors. The Wayside Inn was seemingly in a constant state of remodeling during Taylor's time as owner, though it never affected the popularity of the hotel. Taylor sold the inn in April 1924 to Benjamin Frost. In addition to collecting antiques for the interior and repairing the exterior, Frost began to focus on dining and offered one-dollar steak and chicken dinners. Wayside also began featuring farm-to-table cuisine, as well as homemade jams, jellies and pickles, making it far more than just a hotel. The size of the hotel was becoming a problem, and Frost admitted he had to turn away nearly two dozen people in April 1931 alone. Wayside Inn became a staple of Chatham's dining and lodging scene during the 1930s, with Benjamin Frost being at the front and center. However, he fell into ill health during the 1937 season, which would prove to be his last.

Marjorie Haven bought the hotel from Frost at the beginning of 1938. She did not rest on the reputation of her new business venture—she looked to add to it. In early 1941, an addition to the Wayside was built, enlarging the dining room. During World War II, the U.S. Navy took over the inn, giving housing to servicemen on the Cape. Haven did not stop in her quest to make the Wayside Inn the best it could be during her tenure. She bought the neighboring Harding house and built two cottages. Marjorie emphasized the hotel's lodging and dining equally throughout her ownership. By the time she sold it, the Wayside had grown exponentially.

Virginia and Adam Hart bought the hotel in 1963 and carried the torch for Marjorie Haven into the 1970s. It was expanded to fit two hundred people in the dining room, and the Lantern Lounge and accommodations for eighty people in thirty-five rooms were added. Firmly established as a prime hotel and restaurant, the Wayside was sold to Michael Hickey in 1971. It slipped somewhat during the 1970s and into the 1980s, and it was close to becoming senior housing. Guenther Weinkopf then bought the hotel and renovated it in 1986, saving the property, turning the Lantern Lounge into the Sam Bellamy Tavern and pouring $2 million into it.

Weinkopf eventually ran out of money and sold the hotel to a group that included David Oppenheim in 1993.

Today, the Wayside Inn is an icon of Chatham. After a two-year, multimillion-dollar renovation by David Oppenheim's ownership group and the opening of the Wild Goose Tavern in 2007, this property became firmly entrenched as part of the epicenter of the exquisite Main Street of Chatham. Its award-winning in dining and lodging have achieved levels of success and stability that few businesses are able to find on Cape Cod.

CHEQUESSET INN

ADDRESS: KENDRICK AVENUE, WELLFLEET
YEARS ACTIVE: 1886–1934

On a curve along Kendrick Avenue in Wellfleet, just beyond Mayo Beach, there is a plaque. It is nestled in the shadows of the Wellfleeter Condominiums, and if you're not looking for it, you can pass it by without a thought. However, this plaque was placed in the memory of one of the original bastions of tourism on Cape Cod. It is a reminder of a legendary resort hotel that has long since vanished. It is a tribute to the Chequesset Inn.

The grand resort of the Outer Cape came about through the success of Captain Lorenzo Dow Baker. Baker had struck it rich by importing bananas from Jamaica during the 1870s. Baker created the Boston Fruit Company, which became the United Fruit Company in 1899; it is well known today as Chiquita. During this rise to prominence, Baker built his summer estate, Belvernon, on five acres west of Commercial Street on what is now fittingly Baker Avenue. He continued by purchasing the four-hundred-foot-long Mercantile Wharf located just west of Mayo Beach in 1885.

Wellfleet had been predominantly known as a fishing village in the latter part of the nineteenth century, and as the fishing industry wound down, Baker wanted to increase the town's appeal. He achieved this in spades with the construction of his Hotel Over the Sea, which was christened the Chequesset Inn in 1886. The sixty-two-room, four-story resort quickly turned Wellfleet into a summer resort town. Visitors would mostly arrive via the new spoke of the Old Colony Railroad, which had been finished in 1870. The guests at the Chequesset Inn would be treated to high-end luxury in more than one area. Some of the amenities included both sea and freshwater fishing, boating, tennis, billiards and bowling. The meals included music played by a live orchestra and vegetables grown from the inn's own gardens. Guests could take carriages to nearby ponds or walk down Kendrick Avenue to soak up the sun at Mayo Beach.

By the turn of the twentieth century, Captain Baker had succeeded in making Wellfleet a desirable summer destination. Chequesset changed with the times, bringing in electric lights in the 1890s and welcoming the new automobile crowd during the first decade of the 1900s. Captain Baker also headquartered the Wellfleet Yacht Club at the inn. One of the last contributions of Captain Baker's life came in 1902, when he created the Massachusetts Department of Fisheries Shellfish Laboratory and Quahog Hatchery, also on Mercantile Wharf.

Baker died in 1908 at the age of sixty-eight, with his resort hotel running strong as a booming success. His family took over the day-to-day operations of the resort. The cracks in Chequesset Inn were few, though one began to rear its ugly head. There was no alcohol allowed at the resort, and this became a selling point for new competing resorts like Chatham Bars Inn, which opened in 1914.

As the inn moved into its fourth decade, some physical cracks began to appear. The wharf was being damaged by the harsh New England winters. This problem was alleviated for a time, when, in 1928, lumber was purchased from the recently decommissioned Chatham Naval Station and used to shore up some of the weaknesses at Mercantile Wharf. However, the repairs were not permanent. In February 1934, the sea claimed the Chequesset Inn. After a particularly frigid winter, Wellfleet Harbor was packed with ice. During a strong winter storm, chunks of the ice came free and destroyed parts of the wharf, causing the partial collapse of the inn. Luckily, since the Chequesset Inn was a summer resort, nobody was hurt in the collapse. The Chequesset Inn never reopened, and it was eventually dismantled in September 1934, thus bringing the era of Wellfeet's "grand hotel" to an end.

Today, only memories remain of the Chequesset Inn. It can seem, at times, like the hotel was only a figment of one's imagination. However, physical proof of the old Mercantile Wharf appears, particularly during low tide, when some of the old wharf pilings become visible. Proof of the former Chequesset Inn can also be found. After its demise, some of the lumber was taken by parishioners to Orleans to help create the Church of the Holy Spirit, which still stands today. Otherwise, the Chequesset Inn joins a rather large group of vanished Wellfleet history, alongside Mayo Beach Lighthouse, Billingsgate Island and the Marconi Wireless Station.

COONAMESSETT INN

ADDRESS: 311 GIFFORD STREET, FALMOUTH
YEARS ACTIVE: 1927–PRESENT

Beginning as part of a resort that rose from hundreds of acres of farmland and surviving a move across town at the height of its popularity, the Coonamessett Inn has been indelibly linked with Falmouth for nearly a century. Ahead of its time while also holding on to the history that helped establish it, modern yet old-fashioned, the Coonamessett is far more than just walls and a roof.

The Coonamessett Inn got its name, appropriately, from the pond that lies just to the south of it. Although the inn was part of the town of Falmouth, the pond and the surrounding land resided in an area known as Hatchville. This neighborhood was settled by Jonathan Hatch in 1712. The story of the Coonamessett began nearly a century before its official opening, in 1826, when it was just a farmhouse built by William Chadwick. The farmhouse remained in the family and was rather unassuming through the nineteenth century into the early twentieth century. In 1916, Charles R. Crane, a retired industrialist and summer Woods Hole resident, purchased a large chunk of Hatchville land. He bought the property for Wilfred Wheeler, the former Massachusetts secretary of state and Board of Agriculture member, who ran a modern farm known as the Coonamessett Ranch. Over the next few years, the Crane family purchased more land, bringing the total Coonamessett property up to roughly fifteen thousand acres, and by 1925, it was reported to be the largest farm east of the Mississippi River. During his time as the manager of the Coonamessett Ranch, Wheeler lived in the Chadwick farmhouse. When Wheeler's contract expired in 1925, the farm

The Coonamessett Inn. *Courtesy of Christopher Setterlund.*

business was abandoned after spending a short stint as Brae Burn Farm, and in its place, the idea for a resort took root.

The Coonamessett Ranch Company leased many of the farm buildings in 1927, freeing the company up to create the Coonamessett Inn based in the old Chadwick farmhouse. It was to be the anchor of the larger Coonamessett Resort. A nine-hole golf course was constructed around the converted home, which attracted more visitors to the former farm. There was also a colony of cottages on the property that could be rented for a week or an entire season. After a few uneventful years, a new manager of the fledgling inn changed everything.

In January 1930, the lease of the inn was taken over by Edna Harris, who was already known on Cape Cod. Harris had come to the Cape from Watertown in 1912 and opened the Megansett Tea Room. Her success there prompted the Crane family to reach out. Nine more holes were added to the golf course in 1930, making it a full eighteen-hole course. The hotel also boasted tennis courts, horse stables and both fresh- and saltwater boating.

The Coonamessett Inn saw its popularity rise, and in 1934, a forty-by-thirty-foot addition containing four new bedrooms was built at a cost of $4,000 ($78,500 in 2021). This was only the first addition. In early 1937, a ranch house annex was built with sixteen new rooms. It was ahead of its time, with modern appliances and fireplaces in each room, yet it had an Old West vibe to it. The ranch house was an immediate hit. Harris coupled this success with opening the inn for wedding and dinner parties.

In the 1940s, Coonamessett only got bigger. Ten new cottages were built on the property at the end of 1940. The outbreak of World War II brought many military officials to the inn, as Camp Edwards was located only a few miles away. The entertainment world came to Edna Harris's hostelry during the 1940s as well. In 1949, Richard Aldrich, who ran the Cape Playhouse in Dennis, took over the Coonamessett Club, which had entertained soldiers during World War II. He renamed it the Falmouth Playhouse. The Coonamessett Inn saw many Hollywood celebrities grace its interior, and Edna Harris became a celebrity herself. Despite enjoying more than twenty years of continued success, in August 1953, the Crane family declined to renew Harris's lease on the inn.

The immensely popular Falmouth hotel was leased to Richard Treadway and became one of the fifteen Treadway Inns located across New England, New York and Florida in November 1953. However, Edna Harris was far from defeated. She retained the inn's liquor license, trademarked the Coonamessett name, kept its furniture and took out a lease on the Robert Longyear house on Gifford Street. It took five weeks and constant work to move everything necessary from the old site to the new one. The 150-seat dining room of the new Coonamessett Inn site was filled to capacity on its reopening night, November 24, 1953.

Richard Treadway reopened the former hotel site in the spring of 1954, but it was a failure without the Coonamessett name and charm. By 1957, the Crane family sold the inn to Harvey Clauson. It became Clauson's Inn and Country Club before being sold by the Clauson family in 1977. Today, that area is known as the Cape Cod Country Club.

Edna Harris had taken a chance and continued business as the Coonamessett Inn several miles south of its original location. The risk paid off. In 1954, an antique shop/gift shop annex was built on the property. As Harris reached her eighties, the popularity of her hotel, coupled with her increasing age, brought many suitors who tried to pry the Coonamessett from her. She never sold and retained ownership of the property until her death on January 6, 1967, at the age of eighty-nine. For more than thirty-five years and in two different locations, Edna Harris had become a beloved and respected Cape Cod icon at the Coonamessett. It was a tough act for anyone to follow.

The site of the original Coonamessett Inn. *Courtesy of Christopher Setterlund.*

After Harris's death, her daughter Hilda Harris Coppage arranged for the hotel to be sold to Josiah and Josephine Lilly in 1969. The new owners kept stability at the property for more than twenty years while also adding their own touches. William and Linda Zammer bought the Coonamessett Inn in 1996 for $1 million. They also managed the Flying Bridge Restaurant and had leased the Popponesset Inn in Mashpee, so they were no strangers to hospitality.

In February 2017, the Zammers finalized the sale of the Coonamessett Inn to the boutique hotel company Lark Hotels for $5.55 million. The five-acre property, with its twenty-nine rooms and suites, three-hundred capacity function hall and ninety-seat Eli's Tavern Restaurant, had already been considered luxurious; however, the new ownership made it official. The "Inn" was dropped from its name, and it was completely redesigned as a boutique-style hotel in the heart of Falmouth. Despite its many changes, the decades-old property retains much of its charm from its days under the loving care of Edna Harris.

THE COVE AT YARMOUTH

ADDRESS: 183 ROUTE 28, WEST YARMOUTH
YEARS ACTIVE: 1986–PRESENT

Although the Cove has been home to the high-class of Cape Cod for a little over three decades, the property abutting Mill Creek in West Yarmouth has been drawing in visitors for nearly a century. Long before it was a base camp for travelers, a home for others and, more recently, a hip place to dine and listen to music, this spot along Route 28 was home to a soda shop.

Brad's Soda Shoppe was the idea of Carl Bradshaw. It was built in 1930 as an open-air restaurant, though it was later fully enclosed. The popular establishment relied on tourism, even back in the days before the true boom of Cape Cod. In 1940, it was enlarged, and gas pumps were added, as Carl was anticipating the Cape's popularity going to the next level. It did—but not soon enough for Bradshaw. He sold Brad's Soda Shoppe in 1943, and the new owners rechristened it as a restaurant simply known as Carl's Restaurant. It gained a positive reputation of its own, and it lasted for well over two decades. After Carl's closed, the building itself stood for several years along Route 28 before finally being torn down in 1979. The large empty space along Mill Creek was highly coveted. In March 1984, Malcolm MacPhail of Falmouth and his company, Mill Creek Cove Inc., pitched a proposal for a large hotel. It was actually an altered proposal that they had presented back in June 1974. That original proposal for a 104-room motel and 80-condominium complex on the land owned by Peter Consiglio was approved by the Yarmouth Board of Appeals; yet no construction was done, and the project was dormant.

The entrance to the Cove at Yarmouth. *Courtesy of Christopher Setterlund.*

By the time MacPhail and his company came back to revive the plans for the hotel on Mill Creek, zoning laws had changed, thus the project was denied. Another hurdle was a new motel ban that had been enacted by the town due to the large number of motels in Yarmouth—though the Cove project was not affected, as it was grandfathered in. Construction on the sixty-six rooms at the resort began in mid-1985, and it was known as phase I of the Cove. In addition to the rooms, the property had a sports complex with nine tennis and racquetball courts, a spa, swimming pools and a snack bar. It stretched for hundreds of yards along Route 28, a far cry from the old days of Brad's Soda Shoppe and Carl's Restaurant.

The sixty-six rooms began selling quickly, and soon, ownership sought to change the Cove from a traditional hotel to a hybrid hotel, condominium and timeshare complex. Timesharing was a craze that had become popular in the United States in the early 1970s; it allowed multiple people to purchase a set period of time at a condominium annually. In December 1985, the change to the Cove was approved, with the condition that an on-site wastewater treatment plant would be part of the construction. It was all systems go for the property to be increased to a total of 229 rooms, both hotel rooms and condos, with the option for timesharing.

In a show of good faith and to get some good press among locals, MacPhail offered to turn the seventy-nine-acre site of the former Sandy Pond Club Bar into a recreation area with no strings attached in May 1986. The ownership also agreed to donate roughly half of its twenty-three acres of land to the Conservation Commission around this same time. Construction on the Sandy Pond Recreation Area began in February 1987 at a cost of $500,000 ($1.15 million in 2021) to MacPhail.

The Cove quickly garnered a positive reputation. With the hopes of creating an all-inclusive one-stop resort, MacPhail pushed the hotel's restaurant, first known simply as the Restaurant at the Cove Resort. It became more of a nightspot in 1992, when it became known as the Atrium. The overall experience for guests at the Cove led to its recognition as the best resort on the Mid-Cape by *Cape Cod Life Magazine* in 1993. The late-1990s saw a brief run of Restaurant Pescara inside the Cove; however, it quickly came and went.

In 2006, the Atrium was replaced by a new restaurant known as 4 Bros. Bistro. It was run by Jack and Rocco Collucci, who also ran Collucci Bros. Diner in Hyannis. The restaurant received a bump in visibility when Jack and Rocco were featured on Food Network's *Throwdown! With Bobby Flay* in March 2007. Full-scale renovations followed in 2007–08, with promises to make such improvements routinely.

In 2015, 4 Bros. Bistro closed, with a new restaurant called the Loft opening in 2017. The latest round of renovations occurred in 2017–18 at a cost of $3.5 million, as the ownership, led by longtime general manager Michael Edwards, chooses to never simply rest on its laurels.

Today, the Cove at Yarmouth, with its 229 suites and townhouses, is the largest year-round resort on Cape Cod. Each room is a home away from home, with a separate bedroom and living room, in addition to access to indoor and outdoor pools, a fitness center and more, all under one roof. The Loft and the Loft Shack, which opened in 2018, are the Cove's restaurants and are open to the public. They have garnered their own positive reputations. The resort has combined relaxation and activity seamlessly for more than thirty years. The property has come a long way since the days of Brad's Soda Shoppe before World War II. Centrally located to many attractions, shopping and more, the Cove appears to be on its way to many more years of award-winning service and accommodation.

CUMMAQUID INN

ADDRESS: 2 ROUTE 6A, YARMOUTH PORT
YEARS ACTIVE: 1946–2015

The Cummaquid Inn had a view that could not be beat and a location near the center of the Cape. For decades, the historic estate led a second life as one of the most popular hotels and restaurants Cape Cod had to offer. Although, in later decades, it would be known exclusively as a classy restaurant, in its initial incarnation, it had a mixture of dining and lodging.

The building that would eventually be known as the Cummaquid Inn got its start as the stately home of one of Yarmouth's prominent citizens. Dr. Gorham Bacon, born in Manhattan, New York, in 1855, was a Harvard graduate and highly respected surgeon. He built his own summer home on the Cape in 1893, after visiting numerous times and staying in others' homes. An eighteen-acre plot of land on the border of Barnstable and Yarmouth known as Sunset Heights was chosen as the site of his family estate. The Colonial-style home was completed in September 1893, with Dr. Bacon calling it Matakese. It had views of Mill Pond and Cape Cod Bay that were the envy of most who came to visit. The Bacons had a sort of grand opening party for the locals during the 1894 Fourth of July weekend, and they decked the home out in streamers and flags. Although it was an impressive, stately manor, complete with stables, a greenhouse and several varieties of plants that were not native to Cape Cod, the family never saw the summer home as more than a cottage.

On his retirement in 1920, Dr. Bacon lived full time on Cape Cod until his death in 1940. His home and land were left to his daughter Ruth Cheney and her husband, Austin, who lived in South Manchester, Connecticut.

Anthony's Cummaquid Inn. *Courtesy of Christopher Setterlund.*

Matakese remained in the family as a summer home for several more years. In March 1946, the property was sold to Walter and Martha Scharffe, who had plans to convert the home into an inn. In May, a white sign was erected by the roadside, alerting passersby that the former Matakese estate was to be known as the Cummaquid Hotel. The Scharffes worked tirelessly to get the new business up and running for the summer season. They succeeded, and the new Mid-Cape hotel was opened in June 1946. The first season was considered a big success, and when Cummaquid Hotel closed just after Labor Day, the Scharffes went to Miami Beach for the winter.

After the initial feeling-out process, the Scharffes began to make the Cummaquid Hotel their own. They gave it a fresh coat of white paint, tore down a big barn on the property and built their own small cottage near the property's rose garden in early 1950. Several more cottages were added to the estate, increasing the number of guests who could stay there. The Scharffes also held numerous dinner parties at the hotel, some during the dead of winter, gaining them numerous friends and admirers. In January 1957, a two-bedroom cottage was built on the property.

In January 1963, it was announced that Walter and Martha Scharffe were selling the Cummaquid Hotel to Joseph and Betty Curtis. The couple spent one final season in their personal cottage on the property before moving.

They left behind big shoes for the new owners to fill. The Curtises came aboard after running the Mooring seasonal restaurant on the Hyannis Waterfront for seven years. Where the Scharffes focused mainly on the hotel aspect of the property, the Curtises shifted focus to the restaurant side. The changes began at the top, and the establishment's name was changed to the Cummaquid Inn. The property was reopened on May 30, 1963, with a mix of high-class cuisine and quiet, laid-back lodging.

Despite focusing on the restaurant aspect of the business, Joseph and Betty continued adding lodging options. In April 1964, Joseph had a pair of cottages built on the Yarmouth side of the property after a proposal for six two-bedroom cottages on the Barnstable side was rejected by the town. The new cottages were used for year-round occupancy. In time, Joseph and Betty would add two more cottages and a heated outdoor swimming pool; they also refurbished the existing rooms at the inn. Despite Joseph and Betty's focus on dining, the new cottages would be rented year-round.

In March 1965, the property's age was beneficial to the Curtises. Joseph had a proposal for a fifty-by-thirty-five-foot dining room with three picture windows overlooking Mill Pond approved because the inn had been there before the area's zoning laws existed. It increased the dining room's capacity from fifty to two hundred people. A change from a seasonal to an annual liquor license came in 1967, as Cummaquid Inn remained seasonal but opened for special functions, banquets, weddings and the like. These special events, including the ninetieth birthday of Walter Chase, a retired bank president, in April 1969, which was attended by more than six hundred people, kept the Curtises busy through much of the off season. There was, in reality, very little down time for Joseph and Betty, which began to wear them down.

In May 1973, Joseph and Betty Curtis sold the Cummaquid Inn to Arthur DeSaulniers, who also owned the Gray Gables Ocean House in Bourne. DeSaulniers changed the inn's name to Cummaquid Ocean House, though he kept on most of the Curtises' staff. The inn also finally became a year-round establishment, serving lunch and dinner. DeSaulniers immediately got in trouble when he tried to fill in a hole on the Yarmouth side of the property for parking without a permit. The tenure of DeSaulniers was brief.

In June 1974, the Cummaquid Ocean House was sold to the Anthony's Pier 4 ownership group based out of Boston. Again, the establishment's name was changed, this time to Anthony's Cummaquid Inn. Its dining room was enlarged again by the new owners, as the business had become a popular fine-dining establishment; it was losing touch with its lodging roots.

The changes worked, and Anthony's Cummaquid became a staple for Cape Cod dining well into the twenty-first century.

Anthony's Cummaquid even outlasted Anthony's Pier 4, the ownership's main restaurant in Boston, which was torn down in 2013. However, problems arose around the same time for the Mid-Cape icon. A litany of health inspection violations forced Yarmouth and Barnstable to shut down the restaurant, pending the correction of said violations, at the end of 2015. Despite no official word, as of 2021, Anthony's Cummaquid was dormant and overgrown, with "no trespassing" signs dotting the tree-lined entranceway. If this is its end, it is a sad whisper to a long and storied history that began with Dr. Gorham Bacon and his Matakese estate.

DANIEL WEBSTER INN

ADDRESS: 149 MAIN STREET, SANDWICH
YEARS ACTIVE: MID-1700S–PRESENT

The name Daniel Webster is iconic in Massachusetts. Webster served as the United States secretary of state under three presidents: William Henry Harrison, John Tyler and Millard Fillmore. The famed inn and restaurant that bears his name in historic Sandwich Center has history on Cape Cod even greater than that of Webster. The land on which the Daniel Webster Inn stands today has been home to some sort of establishment for more than 250 years.

The roots of the property at 149 Main Street began in 1692, when it was home to a parsonage that was built for Reverend Roland Cotton. The property was purchased by Reverend Benjamin Fessenden in 1729. Shortly after his death in 1746, Fessenden's son Benjamin Jr. turned the house into a tavern, which competed with the nearby Newcomb Tavern on present-day Grove Street. As the eighteenth century moved on, Fessenden's became a hot spot in Sandwich, as it eventually included a post office and stage stop on the route to Plymouth under its roof. It was during this time that Daniel Webster himself visited the tavern, setting the scene for a big change nearly a century later. The Fessenden family sold the flourishing establishment in October 1831 to General Sabin Smith, who promised to carry on with business as usual.

That changed a few years later, in July 1836, when Smith proclaimed that his establishment was a temperance house, meaning it did not serve alcohol. This change, coupled with a large addition to the building, was all done in the hopes of attracting a clientele of sportsmen from Boston and beyond

The Dan'l Webster Inn. *Courtesy of Christopher Setterlund.*

to come and stay at the property for more than a few hours. The property became known as the Stage Hotel, and Smith worked at promoting this new phase of the establishment until his death in April 1841.

In the years following Smith's death, the property gained the name Central House and was run by a Mr. Scott during the early 1850s. Then John Barker ran the business, beginning in 1858. During these days, the hotel was gaining a reputation as a "famous resort for pleasure-seekers from the city." After Barker's departure in 1860, David Thompson took over. He briefly closed the business and refurnished the house, making small repairs, and then he began promoting high-quality food for the guests once it reopened. However, much like previous owners Scott and Barker, Thompson only stayed for a few years before moving on and leaving the Central House with yet another owner. Despite its relatively frequent ownership changes during the mid- to late nineteenth century, the Central House's popularity only grew, with luminaries such as President Grover Cleveland and writer Henry David Thoreau paying visits.

As the twentieth century dawned, Sandwich's Central House had already become an icon, as it had operated as a high-end hotel and a tavern for nearly seventy years. The food served in the dining area was of great quality, though the emphasis on the cuisine would not come until later. In a bit of foreshadowing, in 1913, the new and final owner of Central House, William McLaughlin, was granted a liquor license. Two years later, things greatly changed.

In August 1915, the Central House was purchased by James McCann and Louis Govoni. They rechristened the legendary establishment the Daniel Webster Inn, and though they maintained it as a hotel, dining still played a small role. The pair then enlarged the building, building an addition on the west end. It quickly became a popular spot for banquets and other important gatherings due to its spacious dining hall. Despite spending time and money on improvements, McCann sold his share in the business in April 1920, as he went off to manage another famed lodging spot, Hotel Attaquin in Mashpee. The Govoni family remained in charge for years to come, even after the sudden death of Louis in 1924.

There was a slow shift at Daniel Webster Inn as the years went on; it began trending more toward the dining and event side and steered away from lodging, which the establishment had been notable for in the previous century. After the end of Prohibition in 1933, the first new liquor license on the Cape in many years fittingly went to this spot, as it had been originally a tavern. By the early 1950s, Daniel Webster Inn, under the leadership of the Govoni family, was being lauded as much for its menu of steak, lobster and chops, along with fancy cocktails, as it was for its lodging accommodations. In the 1960s, the Govoni family sold the iconic establishment to Cheever Newhall, who oversaw the greatest change of all to the business.

On April 17, 1971, a day after Cheever signed the papers to sell the property, a great fire consumed the thirty-room building, destroying the rare antiques, paintings and more that made the location legendary. The loss was estimated to cost $200,000 ($1.29 million in 2021). Despite the outlook seeming grim, the Daniel Webster Inn was not dead.

The new Daniel Webster Inn was rebuilt the very same year, and it was even larger than before. In April 1980, the establishment was purchased by Vincent Catania, the president of Hearth 'n Kettle, for $1 million at auction. Catania created a corporation to manage the inn and restaurant. He upgraded the interior of the property, adding antiques to give it the feel of the original property. It underwent a two-year $2 million renovation between 1998 and 2000, creating a modern inn and restaurant that maintained the charm of its heritage from the Fessenden Tavern, Stage Hotel, Central House and the original Daniel Webster Inn.

Still under the ownership of the Catania family, the restaurant has become an icon in and of itself. It has been recognized in the top 1 percent of restaurants in the country, and it has been designated as a Distinguished Restaurant of North America. The 252-seat Dan'l Webster Inn Restaurant, which has four dining rooms, and the forty-seat tavern at the inn give guests plenty of options when it comes to dining. The forty-eight-room inn is of four-star quality, with a Colonial flare mixing canopy beds and whirlpools. The inn also has the award-winning Beach Plum Spa, which is open to the public, on its premises. With something for all travelers and diners, it is easy to believe that the Daniel Webster Inn will remain a fixture on Cape Cod for decades more to come.

THE EAGLESTON INN

ADDRESS: MAIN STREET, HYANNIS
YEARS ACTIVE: 1910–1960

At the turn of the twentieth century, Hyannis was already seen as a major hub of Cape Cod, although on a smaller scale than it is today. Main Street, which was then lined with trees, was still humming with businesses. A particularly successful entrepreneur of early Main Street was Allen P. Eagleston; his last name became synonymous with Hyannis during the late nineteenth and early twentieth centuries.

Eagleston's first business venture started when he took over the general store that was originally owned by George Thacher on Main Street in April 1883. The Boston Store's huge assortment of goods and low prices guaranteed that it was routinely packed with people. Eagleston was full of energy and ingenuity, with a sense of what was new and exciting as far as products went. His success with the Boston Store would lead to a need for enlargement, so he purchased the adjacent property that was owned by W.E. Foley in 1886. In early 1887, Allen P. Eagleston sold his Boston Store to Prince Crowell and moved to Atlanta, Georgia, to open a similar store called the Bee Hive, which was a failure.

By 1889, Allen and his brother/partner Edward Eagleston were back on Cape Cod. Edward purchased the home of Emily Clark on Main Street in Hyannis in May 1890, and he tore it down to make way for a second incarnation of the Eaglestons store, then called the New York Store. Another opportunity for expansion arose with the construction of the Cash Block Building in 1893. Located at the corner of Main and Pleasant Streets, it became the home of a larger Eagleston store, which occupied the first and second floors of much of the building. The new department store opened on September 27, 1893, to huge fanfare. A second New York Store opened in Vineyard Haven in 1896, and a third opened in Falmouth in 1901. By this time, the Eagleston brothers were big-time players in Cape Cod business.

On December 3, 1904, a large fire destroyed much of the Hyannis Main Street area, including the Eagleston store. The brothers decided to rebuild, and ground was broken on the new Eagleston building at the original spot in February 1905. However, a more appealing plot of land became available farther west on Main Street a month later. The Eaglestons abandoned the idea of rebuilding on the same lot and moved the operation west. Their impressive new Eagleston Shop opened in May 1905. It included a teahouse, and after its first new season, it was quickly enlarged. In November 1908, the teahouse's manager, Claudia Kellogg, purchased the estate of Captain John Winslow Baker, which was then owned by the Eaglestons and also located on Main Street, near its intersection with Bassett Street. Her desire was to turn the mansion into a hotel.

Sadly, in March 1909, just as the renovations were being made, Kellogg suddenly passed away, leading to the sale of the property at auction to Aaron Crosby for $5,750 ($165,000 in 2021). Work continued on the home, although it did not open in 1909. It did open for the 1910 season under the management of K.M. Pinckney and under the name Eagleston Inn. The new hotel was quite successful from the beginning, as it piggybacked off of the success of the Eagleston brothers' other ventures on Main Street. The piazzas of the hotel were enlarged after the 1911 season as part of extensive improvements that were being made. Margaret and Mary Wiley took the reins for the 1912 season.

Edward Eagleston died suddenly in August 1913 at the age of fifty-three. Despite this loss, the Eagleston name garnered more notoriety with the emergence of another brother, James. He would take control of the Eagleston Inn from the Wileys in 1914.

Allen Eagleston died in 1917 at the age of sixty-one, leaving James to carry the ball from his brothers on his own. James did this by adding a dance pavilion to Eagleston Inn in April 1919. The dancing and dining hall made the property much more than just a hotel. Over time, though, James Eagleston grew weary of the constant work of running a popular hotel, not to mention the rest of the Eagleston properties. In May 1922, Eagleston sold the inn to Morgan S. Dada.

By the 1924 season, Dada had found his footing, and the Eagleston Inn became not only a popular seasonal hotel but a hot spot for dinner in the

White Room and dancing every afternoon and night. The dancing aspect was led by Chet Copp and the Eagleston Inn Orchestra. This group made history as one of the first musical acts on Cape Cod's first radio station, WSGC, which existed briefly from July to September 1926. The dining aspect of the hotel was highlighted by its scrumptious chicken dinners, as well as its porch tearoom, which was perfect for summer activities. It was reported that the hotel routinely served 100 breakfasts and as many as 350 dinners at the peak of its season. Although James Eagleston died in 1928, the hotel that bore his family's name continued its success into the 1930s.

Main Street in Hyannis, however, was beginning to change and become more modern. At the end of 1936, the Eagleston Inn Annex, which housed a few shops, was torn down to make way for a newer building. An interesting event took place on August 30, 1937, when Dora Baker Emery hosted a dinner party at the Eagleston. Dora's grandfather was John Winslow Baker, who had originally built the home. In fact, her father, brother and nephew had all been born in the same room where the party was held.

In January 1938, Morgan Dada was foreclosed on by the bank, and the Eagleston Inn was taken over by the Hyannis Trust. Shortly thereafter, Carl Holm, the owner of the Viking Restaurant in Boston, purchased the inn. Major changes came quickly. Holm introduced a terrace garden in front of the hotel, and most importantly, he constructed the Viking Restaurant inside the Eagleston, complete with a Swedish smorgasbord. Holm pushed the Viking Restaurant aspect of the Eagleston, although the property was closed during World War II, as Holm had entered naval intelligence. On reopening, the restaurant's service changed, as it had become too expensive to import foods for the smorgasbord.

An advertisement for Eagleston Inn from 1922. *Courtesy of Project Gutenberg.*

The Eagleston Inn was the site of the afterparty for the opening night of the Cape Cod Music Circus (later known as the Melody Tent) on July 4, 1950. After Holm's death in 1958, his wife, Idale, continued to run the property. In February 1960, the Eagleston Inn and its surrounding property was purchased by Manuel Koufman and Samuel Poorvu from Boston. They continued the modernization of Main Street by building a newer shopping center. Idale Holm had grand plans to move the Eagleston Inn and Viking Restaurant out to West Main Street; however, her plans were quashed after her death in September 1961. It was a quiet exit for the Eagleston Inn, though its name and legacy live on in the form of the Eagleston Wing of the Hyannis Library, which was built in 1939 with funds that had been allocated by Edward Eagleston before his death in 1913. This means that, even though Main Street—and Hyannis, in general—has changed immeasurably in the ninety years since the last Eagleston brother died, their name is still spoken among the modern restaurants and shops that dot the hub of Cape Cod.

EAST BAY LODGE

ADDRESS: 199 EAST BAY ROAD, OSTERVILLE
YEARS ACTIVE: 1886–1998

A century is a long time—longer than the lifespan of most humans. Few business enterprises last more than a few years, let alone over one hundred. However, the longevity established by East Bay Lodge, as both a hotel and a restaurant, allowed it to create memories spanning across several generations. This icon of Cape Cod has housed weddings, banquets, private functions and birthdays, and it has also given visitors a place to rest their heads in between sunny days of exploring the Cape.

The legacy of East Bay Lodge goes all the way back to the latter part of the nineteenth century. The lodge was built by Nelson H. Bearse Jr. in 1886. Bearse had gone to sea at the age of twenty-two, and he captained a schooner called the *Nelson Harvey*. The inn was created from Nelson and his wife, Mary's, home, which overlooked the peaceful East Bay and Nantucket Sound. It was originally the home of Bearse's grandfather Thomas Ames, and it stood on the grounds of an old saltworks. The village of Osterville, from the start, was a prime resort area, attracting people from all over America. With so much room in their home, it was only natural for the Bearses to accommodate visitors. In 1890, an extensive remodeling job was done on the Bearses' home, turning it from a good-sized family home into the glorious inn that would become one of the finest in all of New England. After only a decade, rave reviews of the inn's décor and amenities flowed in from gaggles of satisfied travelers. Another expansion occurred in 1900, when the neighboring Josiah Ames homestead was turned sideways and

East Bay Lodge. *Courtesy of the Sturgis Library.*

incorporated into the lodge. In 1911, another annex, including a fifty-foot-tall tower, was constructed to house the growing staff.

The twentieth century dawned, and the popularity of East Bay Lodge only grew. It became the place to be for vacationers, rivaling all of the other inns and resorts along the East Coast. Once it opened for the season, the arrivals at the lodge would be posted throughout the local newspapers. Guests could walk the beautiful grounds, traverse the flower gardens, find a cozy nook to relax in the shade of a tree or simply stare at boats passing by and breathe in the salty air. For fun, there was golf, tennis, croquet, fishing, boating and swimming to be had. East Bay grew to be more of an estate with time, boasting multiple buildings and seventy-five rooms. It was meant to be a home away from home, with guests rarely staying for one night; more often, they would stay for weeks or months. However, not all of those who wished to stay there had the means to do so; for these guests, there was another side to East Bay Lodge.

Inside, the elegant resort was home to some of the most exquisite fine dining Cape Cod had to offer. From its décor to its cuisine, East Bay Lodge took on a whole new life for those who came to dine there. The interior of the dining room was dotted with beautiful oriental rugs over its hardwood floors. Each table was adorned with white tablecloths, fine china and silver. It was a feast for the eyes before food was even thought of. Fine dining meant formal dress; men had to wear jackets, while women had to wear dresses or formal pantsuits. Though it would change over time, the menu always catered to the finest tastes. Swordfish, cod, scallops, lamb, prime rib, filet mignon and a wide array of wines were available for guests of the hotel and those who came to simply enjoy an elegant dinner. Guests could even find unique delicacies like shad roe and frog legs on the menu at times. Vegetables from the hotel's garden were used to make some of these sumptuous meals.

Once the Bearses retired in April 1917, East Bay was taken over by Charles Brown and Forrest Toward from Revere. The Bearses then moved to Providence. Brown was, at one point, the president of the Cape Cod, Martha's Vineyard and Nantucket Hotel Association. The hotel experienced some close calls with disaster, like the fire in May 1923, which was luckily contained with very minimal damage. In May 1924, Brown became the hotel's sole owner, and he continued to make it the place to be until he sold it and retired in May 1943. Sadly, Brown died in December that same year in Swampscott. The powerhouse Cape Cod establishment was then purchased by F.L. Putnam, the head of the Buzzards Bay Gas Company.

East Bay Lodge stood among the giants of the hospitality industry of the early twentieth century, like the Chequessett Inn in Wellfleet and Wianno Club in Osterville. Its popularity allowed it to become a year-round business, as it became a hotspot for banquets, weddings, private parties and holiday gatherings. Bob and Janel Kesten moved to Osterville and took over East Bay in 1965, promoting the dining side of the inn as much as the hotel, garnering a year-round liquor license for the iconic establishment. Janel shockingly died in 1967, leaving Bob to tend to the business on his own for a while.

Bob introduced nightly entertainment and dancing to add a little more flare to the well-established lodge. Kesten battled the town for several years over the lodge's year-round status, eventually winning in 1972. Then he was allowed to renovate the grounds and rent out twenty rooms on a year-round basis, though he was not allowed to carry out a larger expansion of the property. Catering also helped bring the East Bay experience to places outside of the grounds. Shellfish buffets, fabulous roast beef, Sunday brunch and a constant finger on the pulse of yesteryear kept this spot pumping out satisfied guests and customers as it reached its one hundredth year. Francis Ricci joined the ownership a few years after the Kesten family.

In February 1985, East Bay was sold to John Voros and Bud Ente for $2.5 million ($6.1 million in 2021). The new management desired to increase the number of rooms at the lodge threefold, from eighteen to fifty-four, and add a thirty-by-fifty-foot enclosed pool. They wanted to do all of this

Various scenes from East Bay Lodge. *Courtesy of the Sturgis Library.*

while keeping up the high quality of the cuisine the restaurant offered. By this time, East Bay Lodge was getting 75 percent of its income through the restaurant. The proposal to add more rooms was ultimately denied.

East Bay Lodge continued its successful run through the rest of the 1980s and well into the 1990s, becoming a landmark that had seemingly always existed. Sadly, all good things must come to an end, which was the case with East Bay Lodge. After serving and delighting innumerable guests for over a century, the restaurant was shuttered in 1996. It was run as an inn by Jim Crocker for two more years while he made plans to replace it with luxury townhouses. The final event in the history of the East Bay Lodge was a political rally that took place on August 2, 1998. Shortly thereafter, the lodge was demolished and replaced by the Cove at East Bay, which was still standing as of 2021.

To this day, people still wistfully think back to their past visits to East Bay Lodge. From its roots as a sea captain's home through its initial expansion and gradual conversion into restaurant powerhouse, the establishment always strove for the highest-quality experience for its guests. For over one hundred years, East Bay Lodge not only bred respect and created memories, it was one of the most beloved spots on the Cape for countless diners and travelers alike.

GRAY GABLES INN

ADDRESS: 217 PRESIDENTS ROAD, BOURNE
YEARS ACTIVE: 1925–1973

Gray Gables Inn began its life as the first summer White House, which belonged to President Grover Cleveland. Decades later, the beautiful estate that overlooked Buzzards Bay experienced a second chapter as a popular inn. It was known as Gray Gables and, later, the Gray Gables Inn.

In the twentieth and twenty-first centuries, several presidents of the United States spent time on Cape Cod. Barack Obama and Bill Clinton both took vacations in Martha's Vineyard, while John F. Kennedy stayed at his family's compound in Hyannis Port. Several other sitting presidents have visited the Cape and its islands, including Ulysses S. Grant, Theodore Roosevelt and William Taft. Grover Cleveland, the only president to serve two nonconsecutive terms, fell in love with Cape Cod during his first term (1885–89). His family rented a home in the nearby town of Marion and visited the Cape frequently with his friend and actor Joseph Jefferson. Jefferson was well known for his role as fictional character Rip Van Winkle, both on stage and, in 1896, in one of the earliest motion pictures.

In May 1890, after visiting Joseph Jefferson's summer home on Buttermilk Bay in Wareham, Grover Cleveland decided to make a purchase. He chose the town of Bourne, where he had previously enjoyed fishing, as the site of his new home. The home that he purchased for $20,000 ($575,000 in 2021) was located along the Monument River, at the end of present-day Presidents Road, on 112 acres of land. It was built in 1880 and had been named Tudor Haven after the Tudor family who had originally owned it. Cleveland renamed the home Gray Gables and spent his first summer there in 1891.

A postcard of the Gray Gables Inn. *Courtesy of the Bourne Historical Society.*

In 1892, Grover Cleveland was elected president for a second time, and Gray Gables became the first summer White House on Cape Cod. That same year, out of necessity, a small railroad station was built half a mile away, on Monument Neck Road, to assure fast service back to Washington, D.C. Cleveland also had a telephone line installed in 1892. The duties of the presidency did not stop Cleveland's love of Cape Cod, and he continued to find as much time as possible to visit Gray Gables in Bourne.

Cleveland served his second term from 1893 to 1897, and he retired after leaving the White House. However, two events occurred that cut Cleveland's dream of retiring to Cape Cod short. In 1904, Cleveland's daughter Ruth died of diphtheria at the age of thirteen. It was around this same time that rumors began to swirl about the possibility of a Cape Cod Canal being dug, passing through the backyard of Gray Gables. Not wanting to deal with years of construction close by and heartbroken over the death of his daughter, Grover Cleveland made the summer of 1904 his last on Cape Cod. The family rented out Gray Gables after that. Grover Cleveland died in 1908, with his son Richard selling Gray Gables in 1920. The property's most famous tenant may have moved out, but the story of Gray Gables was far from over.

In 1922, Brown and Stackpole bought the entire site with the intention of subdividing it for residential properties. The three-story Gray Gables was left intact, and in 1925, it made its debut as a lodging alternative. The new hotel kept much of the furnishings and charm from when it was the summer White House, contributing to its allure to travelers.

By 1926, fifty houses had been built on the sprawling property, making it a very desirable waterfront neighborhood. The property and former president were so beloved that the entire neighborhood took on the name Gray Gables. The Gray Gables Inn was managed by John Stackpole and his wife, Jane, for more than ten years, though they did take 1936 off, allowing C. Tracy Ryan to run it for a season. The inn could accommodate up to thirty people, and it had a dining area with a cocktail lounge as well. The inn had delectable food and drink, with room for eighty in the dining room and another fifty in the cocktail lounge. The Stackpoles allowed private parties and banquets to use the large dining and cocktail areas, giving Gray Gables a community feel in Bourne.

Jane Stackpole's death in 1942 spelled the end of the family's operation of the property. It was then sold to Ralph Samuelson and Patricia Smith, who ran it until 1951, when it was sold to Thomas Byrd Epps. Epps successfully petitioned the town to have gas pumps installed at the end of the 160-foot pier that stood on the 750 feet of private waterfront land of Gray Gables. Under the guidance of Epps, Gray Gables continued its push to be one of the most popular summer resorts on Cape Cod. There was an increased promotion of the tremendous fishing that had made the area so attractive to President Cleveland in the first place, along with boating and swimming at the private beach.

In April 1958, Henry Tisdell of Shrewsbury purchased Gray Gables from Epps for $45,000 ($407,000 in 2021). Tisdell also bought 52,500 square feet of land at the site where Gray Gables had originally stood. Immediately, Tisdell formed Gray Gables Inn Inc. The new owner planned to keep the seasonal establishment virtually unchanged, except for minor redecoration, and he strove to continue providing excellent lodging and cuisine to travelers. In the summer of 1959, the past met the present when one of Grover Cleveland's grandsons came to visit Gray Gables. He was given a tour by Tisdell, and he was able to view some of his grandfather's artifacts that still remained there, including his writing desk that sat in the lobby and his fishing equipment.

Despite achieving a positive reputation and standing in the community, the Gray Gables Inn changed hands again in the summer of 1961. Peggy Alden, with an extensive hotel and restaurant background, bought the property with the desire to keep it unchanged. Perhaps Alden's greatest

The near-replica home at the location where Gray Gables Inn once stood. *Courtesy of Christopher Setterlund.*

addition to the legacy of Gray Gables was the outings for children that she arranged. These outings allowed dozens of underprivileged children a day to enjoy the beauty of the seaside property.

Gray Gables continued to enthrall visitors with the charm of its interior, its pristine views of the Cape Cod Canal and its exquisite cuisine for another decade. It was purchased in the early 1970s by Arthur DeSaulniers, who also went on to buy the Cummaquid Inn. On December 10, 1973, a suspicious fire destroyed the Gray Gables Inn, which was known as Gray Gables Ocean House at the time. It was a total loss, amounting to $500,000 ($2.94 million in 2021). It took one hundred firefighters three hours to extinguish the blaze, bringing the story of Cape Cod's first summer White House to a sad end. Perhaps even sadder was the fact that the property that had housed Gray Gables remained vacant and overgrown for nearly thirty years.

At the turn of the twenty-first century, a private home was built at the end of Presidents Road by a couple from Worcester. It was nearly a replica of the original Gray Gables. Though it is no longer a hotel, boats that pass by along the Cape Cod Canal can gaze on it and hearken back to how the landscape looked when Grover Cleveland called it home. The old Gray Gables Railroad Station still stands on the grounds of the Aptucxet Trading Post Museum, only a little more than a mile east of where it once dropped President Grover Cleveland off.

HIGHLAND HOUSE

ADDRESS: SOUTH HIGHLAND ROAD /
HIGHLAND LIGHT ROAD, TRURO
YEARS ACTIVE: 1861–1969

The little town of Truro, with a population of 1,580, according to 2017 Census Bureau data, packs natural beauty and history into its borders. Perhaps no spot encapsulated the quiet charm of old Cape Cod for travelers like the Highland House. Situated just steps away from the historic Highland Lighthouse, near the bluffs and with amazing views of the Atlantic Ocean, Highland House's legacy spanned more than a century and two totally separate buildings.

The property that became Highland House began as land that belonged to prosperous farmer Isaac Small. After his death in 1816, the farmland was divided between Small's two sons, Joshua and James. In 1835, James Small built a farmhouse on his land east of South Highland Road. James and his son Isaac Morton served as the keepers of Highland Lighthouse for decades; the land on which it had been built was originally owned by James's father, Isaac. When James took over as the keeper of the lighthouse, he moved his family into the keeper's house, leaving his father's farmhouse usually unoccupied.

Henry David Thoreau paid four visits to Cape Cod (1849, 1850, 1855 and 1857), and he made his way to Truro each time. Thoreau spent the night each time at the keeper's house with James Small and his family. During one of his trips, James remarked that his farmhouse had room for several boarders. Though he was not specifically advertising rooms for rent at the time, the Highland House was born rather unspectacularly during the years just prior to the Civil War.

The popularity of Cape Cod as a tourist destination, thanks, in part, to Thoreau's masterpiece *Cape Cod*, published in 1865, made boardinghouses like the Smalls' necessary. Highland House was first mentioned in local newspapers as the site of a raucous Fourth of July party in 1865. Business saw a tremendous upswing with the extension of the railroad line all the way to Provincetown in 1873. The hotel was routinely filled throughout the summer season. Morton Small took over the property after his father's death in February 1874. In 1876, to take advantage of the increasing tourism, a two-story wing was added to the farmhouse, more than doubling its size. The rates were reasonable for such a desirable location, either $1 a day or $7 for a week ($24.45 and $171 in 2021, respectively).

Morton had travelers picked up at the railroad station and taken to the hotel via horse-drawn carriages. Though he initially lived inside the Highland House, Morton built his own house, called Cliff House, just north of Highland Lighthouse in 1880. This left the hotel to be used simply as a business. More renovations and improvements came in 1880, including a fresh coat of paint. In addition to its rooms and meals, Highland House would host dances throughout the season. Sometimes they were held inside with a band, and other times, they were held outside, making use of the farmland and windmill on the property.

Even into the 1880s, Morton Small kept up with the family farm but in a diminished capacity. He kept turkeys, chickens and horses on the property, balancing the rural farm life with the rising popularity of the hotel. Small continued to try to balance his work-to-life ratio by maintaining the ownership of Highland House, but he brought in other people to lease it and manage it for him in the late 1880s and early 1890s. In 1894, Small had a grand plan to subdivide the rest of his family's land in order to build a community of cottages in the area surrounding Highland House. The idea was a failure, as few lots were sold after a few years. Truro's year-round population at the turn of the twentieth century was only 767. Rather than continue to push the subdivision idea, Small changed course and decided to add to his hotel holdings. Three large cottages were built on the land: Millstone in 1898 and the Rock and Beacon in 1902. The summer seasons continued to be successful for Morton Small, with the capacity of the property routinely reaching seventy people. Still, the increasing tourist season led to an increased demand for rooms to rent, and with Highland House maxed out at forty rooms, Small decided, in 1906, to build a new hotel.

In May 1906, work began on the new hotel, which was tentatively known as the Highland House Annex. It was located only one hundred yards from the original Highland House. Morton Small himself updated readers about the progress through the columns he wrote in the *Provincetown Advocate* between 1906 and 1907. The new, larger building was virtually complete before the 1907 tourist season. In a move that caused much confusion among the guests, the new hotel was referred to as Highland House, despite the original being a stone's throw away. The original hotel was renamed Highland Lodge in 1909. The new Highland House had a large piazza from which the dinner bell would ring. The new hotel had easier access to the beach, as it had a staircase that led guests down the cliffs. The property even had a bowling alley.

The "Haven" cottage was added in 1915, along with the interesting "Ship" cottage. The Ship cottage was the former deck house of a barge called *Coleraine*, which had run aground near Highland Lighthouse. It was somehow hauled up the cliffside and fashioned into a five-room cottage. The final pieces of the Highland estate were the "Margaret Adams" cottage, added in 1917; the "Pilgrim" cottage (a former general store), added in 1920; and the "Mayflower" cottage, added in 1928.

The increased prevalence of automobiles changed the way resorts like Highland House were run; stays were shorter, and a large garage was added to the property, replacing the horse stable, in 1925. After Morton Small's death in 1934, his only surviving daughter, Lillian, gained ownership of much of the property. It remained in the Small family until June 1947, when it was purchased by Eddie Mayo, the second baseman of the Detroit Tigers, and former minor-league baseball player Hal Conklin. The pair reopened the property shortly after purchasing it, as it had been closed down during World War II. Some big changes were made, including opening the dining room to the public, allowing Highland House to run as a hotel and restaurant. As fewer guests came to stay at the hotel, focus shifted to playing the Highland Links and visiting the lighthouse, and Conklin gravitated toward selling souvenirs and snacks closer to the lighthouse. The big plans for modernizing the property did not materialize due to a lack of funds. It appeared the hotel's time was running out. The original Highland House was sold and moved to Old County Road in South Truro in 1962.

The creation of the Cape Cod National Seashore in 1961 further complicated the status of the Highland House. Hal Conklin, who was, by then, the sole owner, sold the property to the National Park Service in July 1964. He retained the right to continue operating Highland House for three years and an additional option for two more after that. The rights were transferred to Conklin's former employees Joe Colliano and Bill Hastings.

The Highland House Museum. *Courtesy of Christopher Setterlund.*

The pair continued operating Highland House as both a hotel and restaurant through 1969. After that, it was saved from razing when it became a museum and home to the Truro Historical Society. It still stands today along the Highland Links Golf Course and in the shadow of Highland Light, a reminder of the dawn of the tourist boom on Cape Cod that occurred more than a century ago.

HOTEL ATTAQUIN

ADDRESS: ROUTE 130, MASHPEE
YEARS ACTIVE: 1840–1955

The Native Mashpee Wampanoag Tribe is engrained in the history of Cape Cod as much any group can be. They were living on the Cape before the first European settlers explored the area; they even helped the Pilgrims survive their first winter after they arrived in Plymouth in 1620.

The town of Mashpee has been filled with great members of the Wampanoag Tribe; they have not only been leaders for their people but for the town as well. They have held offices and important jobs and become legends in the history of Mashpee and Cape Cod. Some, like legendary former Wampanoag chief "Flying Eagle," Earl Mills Sr., owned restaurants in town, like his iconic Flume, which he ran from 1972 to 2004. Others provided lodging, none more beloved and remembered than the Hotel Attaquin, which spent a century carving out a legacy.

The Hotel Attaquin was brought to life by Wampanoag Tribe member Solomon Attaquin, who became just as well-known as his establishment. Born in 1810, Attaquin went to sea by the age of twelve, visiting Europe and the West Indies while serving as a cook and whaler, among other things, and rising to the rank of mate. At the age of twenty-four, Attaquin returned home to begin a new chapter of his life, and by 1839, he had purchased a plot of land in Mashpee, where he built a home. Within a year, and after a few suitable additions, the home was renamed Hotel Attaquin.

The seventeen-room hotel on ten acres of land quickly became popular as a home base for sportsmen of the day. There was great fishing on the 737 acres of Mashpee and Wakeby Ponds that were located only a few hundred yards north of the hotel. The first big name to make Hotel Attaquin a regular stop was Daniel Webster. Serving as the United States secretary of state under presidents William Henry Harrison, John Tyler and Millard Fillmore, Webster frequented the hotel so much that a room was eventually named after him.

Not resting on the burgeoning success of his hotel, Solomon Attaquin became a fixture in the village of Mashpee. He served as a selectman for twenty-one years, and he served as a treasurer for sixteen years. In 1871, the village of Mashpee was incorporated as a town, with Attaquin being named the first postmaster in January. There was no rail line into Mashpee, so at first, the incoming mail was collected in Sandwich and brought to Hotel Attaquin, which doubled as the post office.

Holding jobs like treasurer, selectman and postmaster stretched Solomon Attaquin too thin. He was unable to focus all of his attention on his lodging establishment, though closing it during the winter did help. In April 1888, at the age of seventy-eight, Attaquin sold his eponymous hotel. The new owner, Oliver Holmes, had frequented the hotel for years when visiting from his home of Francestown, New Hampshire. Holmes also took over the reins of postmaster from Solomon in 1889, though he only held that title for a year before the title was taken by Lysander Amos, who also moved the post office to his home on Great Neck Road North.

Holmes made Hotel Attaquin his main purpose, building an addition in 1888 and pushing it to even greater heights. The improvements to the hotel attracted more legendary names, like President Grover Cleveland, Massachusetts governor William Russell and actor Joseph Jefferson, all avid fishermen.

Solomon Attaquin continued to live on his land, selling small parcels at auction before passing away in March 1895 at the age of eighty-five. He was Mashpee's oldest resident at the time of his passing, and he was one of its greatest success stories. His successor at the hotel, Oliver Holmes, also became well known in Mashpee by continuing the success of the establishment, running several local cranberry bogs and purchasing the nearby trout brooks. Holmes was on hand when Hotel Attaquin received its first telephone line in 1901. He also added an icehouse, clam house and garage to the premises.

Shortly after the turn of the twentieth century, in April 1903, Holmes passed away suddenly at the age of seventy, leaving the hotel to be run by his estate until it was sold to Joseph Peters in 1909. It was during this period that Hotel Attaquin began opening its doors for dinner. In the 1920s, the hotel reached new heights with advertising in the local newspapers. There were traditional clambakes during the summer, along with steak, chicken and lobster dinners prepared by well-known chef Fred Gray. The hotel had become one of the Upper Cape's swinging hot spots.

The news was not all good though. In April 1928, during the height of Prohibition, state police were tipped off and raided Hotel Attaquin. Inside, they found illegal gambling in the form of dice games and alcohol. In all, eight quarts of various liquors were confiscated, along with three gaming machines. Nine people were arrested, including then-owner Ann McCann; though five of the arrested individuals were released after paying fines of five dollars ($76.49 in 2021).

In the ensuing years, the establishment regained its popularity, eventually receiving a proper liquor license after Prohibition was repealed. Under owner Patrick Murphy, the property saw new success. This success was credited to Manning Francis and his Hotel Attaquin Orchestra being featured on WOCB Radio three nights a week in the early 1940s. Former Mashpee police chief Louis Mills was even brought in to be the chef.

Mashpee Community Garden on the site of the former Hotel Attaquin. *Courtesy of Christopher Setterlund.*

The story of Hotel Attaquin had a tragic ending. On the night of December 17, 1955, only a few hours after a Christmas party had been held at the hotel, a fire broke out near the rear entrance to the kitchen. The electrical fire, which was caused by an overloaded outlet, spread quickly. Fire departments from Mashpee, Falmouth, Cotuit and Otis Air Force Base were called in; however, the problem was exacerbated by the fact that Mashpee had no town water system, and the temperature that night was purported to be sixteen degrees Fahrenheit. Firemen had to break through ice in nearby ponds to get water to try to put out the blaze, but it was not to be. Hotel Attaquin burned to the ground, sadly taking the lives of two airmen from Otis.

The hotel's legacy was carved out over more than a century from its beginnings as the home of Mashpee Wampanoag legend Solomon Attaquin to its final chapter as a swinging hot spot with a restaurant and orchestra. Though there may be nothing left of this icon but photographs and fading memories, its importance to the history of Mashpee and Cape Cod will never fade. Today, the Mashpee Community Gardens are located roughly where Hotel Attaquin once stood.

HOTEL BELMONT

ADDRESS: 1 BELMONT ROAD, WEST HARWICH
YEARS ACTIVE: 1894–1974

The time around the turn of the twentieth century was a fork in the road of the evolution of Cape Cod. Until that time, the majority of the economy of the Cape was powered by the fishing and whaling industries. It was during the last few decades of the nineteenth century that the idea of Cape Cod as a summer vacation destination began to take shape. As the Cape grew in popularity, a string of lavish, beautiful resorts began to spring up all over the peninsula. During this time, the Mid-Cape area was devoid of resorts; however, that would change, thanks to the vision of a Civil War veteran and magazine entrepreneur.

Benjamin Johnson came to Cape Cod from South Reading, Massachusetts, in the early 1890s. Johnson had fought in the Union navy during the Civil War before finding another calling. In 1877, Johnson created the *New England Grocer* magazine, which ran weekly. He purchased another magazine, the *New England Druggist*, in 1891. In time, *New England Grocer* became the largest and most respected grocery trade journal in the United States. Johnson was a pioneer in the industry. That pioneer spirit led him to take another risk.

In 1894, Johnson partnered with his friend Caleb Chase, a West Harwich resident, to find a site for a summer resort, which the Mid-Cape needed to keep up with the blossoming tourism industry. They found such a location at the mouth of the Herring River, on the Harwich–Dennis town line. The twenty-two-acre lot was the perfect place. It had pristine beachfront property on the calmer Nantucket Sound, it was centrally located near the area's businesses and it was an easy trip from the railroad station.

A postcard of the Belmont Hotel. *Courtesy of the Boston Public Library.*

The construction of the resort was quick and painless. The new venture, called Hotel Belmont, was ready for business on July 4, 1894. It was a three-and-a-half-story, rectangular wooden structure capable of comfortably housing between 200 and 225 guests at a time. The resort offered amenities such as horseback riding, bowling, fishing and, of course, bathing in the beach that was only a short walk away. It also held concerts and dances in its casino ballroom, and it held dinners with live orchestras. One first that came from Hotel Belmont was a stock market ticker-tape machine in the lobby; nothing like it had been seen on Cape Cod previously. This item earned the Belmont the nickname of "Summer Wall Street."

The seasonal resort was so successful from the start that Johnson was almost immediately looking for ways to expand it. But that would have to wait. In the meantime, the scenery that surrounded Hotel Belmont became more picturesque with the addition of Chatham's Kendrick Windmill, which was moved across the river from the resort at Old Mill Point in 1895; it still stands there today.

After 1908, the hotel's fourteenth successful season, Benjamin Johnson pitched big plans to add forty new rooms to Hotel Belmont. Again, the plans had to wait. However, the wait this time was much shorter; in December 1912, a new three-story cottage and enlarged garage were added to the property. By this time, the summer tourism industry was growing with the rise of the automobile, and tourists were bringing their vehicles to the area for sightseeing.

Johnson bought out his partners and took full control of Hotel Belmont in 1916. He continued to run the property in the same way; although he did sell items, such as all of the carriages that were used to pick people up from the train station, as they were becoming obsolete. His reign as the sole owner was short-lived. In April 1917, Johnson died at the age of seventy-four, leaving control of the resort to his wife and son Benjamin Jr. Sadly, Benjamin Jr. died two years later at the age of thirty-six, and Johnson's wife passed in 1927.

The resort was then run by Johnson's daughter Susan Ulm until her death in 1941, after which it was run by a trusteeship until 1958, when it was bought by longtime guests Edmund Taylor and Robert Baldwin. It was around this time that Hotel Belmont, an icon of its time, became regarded as the "Aristocrat of Cape Cod Hotels."

Despite its run of success, there was one thing Hotel Belmont could not overcome: fire. On November 3, 1974, Harwich Fire Department responded to a small grass fire on the property of the Belmont around 9:45 p.m. It was quickly extinguished. However, less than an hour later, they were called back, this time, for a much larger structural fire. It was naturally seen as very suspicious, and though the property was ultimately saved that night, it was never reopened. There were tentative plans in 1976 to restore Hotel Belmont, but they never were fulfilled, and the legendary resort was torn down in 1977. Ironically, a fire had nearly taken the resort down decades before. In November 1931, a fire destroyed Ms. Elizabeth Heggarty's boardinghouse nearby; at that time, firefighters were able to keep the flames from the resort.

Three years after its demolition, the Belmont was rebuilt as a group of luxury condos. As of 2021, they were still standing, overlooking Nantucket Sound, much like the "Summer Wall Street" had for about eighty years.

HOTEL CHATHAM

ADDRESS: FOX HILL ROAD, CHATHAM
YEARS ACTIVE: 1890–1910

For generations, Cape Cod has been one of the nation's premiere vacation destinations. Its population routinely swells 250 percent every summer. However, this was not always the case. There was a time when Cape Cod was a place where the noise barely rose above a whisper. There was a time when businesses only dreamed of bringing more people to these shores. This time was the late nineteenth century—long before television or even radio advertising. It was a time before automobiles and paved roads, when trains ruled transportation.

As the 1800s drew to a close, the desire to make the Cape more appealing to tourists reached a fevered pitch. An idea was pitched that was to be a first on the peninsula: a luxury resort hotel. Today, places like Wequassett, Chatham Bars Inn, Ocean Edge and others attract people with their spectacular rooms, amenities, views and more, but 130 years ago, lodging on Cape Cod was simple, and the idea of a mammoth luxury resort was foreign.

The concept of such a resort was brought to the forefront in 1889 by the Chatham Real Estate Trust, led by the future owner of Jordan Marsh Eben Dyer Jordan and Edward Taft, the president of the New York & Boston Dispatch Express Company. They had chosen a peninsula in Chatham Port known as Nickerson Neck for development. The groundbreaking ceremony for the resort that would be appropriately named Hotel Chatham took place in July 1889. A few months later, in November 1889, construction began. Newspapers at the time reported that more than 150,000 bricks

Hotel Chatham. *Courtesy of the Sturgis Library.*

were used for the building's masonry. The buildup ahead of the opening included the publication of a twenty-three-page pamphlet, complete with a concept art sketch of the future Hotel Chatham; these pamphlets were sent out to build interest.

On February 11, 1890, the *Chatham Monitor* had this to say about Hotel Chatham's impending opening: "It looks like a thing of beauty, and we hope it will be a joy forever to the stockholders. It will, without doubt, be one of the finest buildings in this part of the state when completed." The obstacle of the hotel's seclusion was combated by the construction of a new railroad station in West Chatham, which took prospective guests out to the resort via railway.

The hype and high praise that surrounded the project led to a successful grand opening in July 1890, with the thirty-thousand-square-foot hotel costing a total of $150,000 ($4.3 million in 2021). With three stories and more than seventy rooms, hundreds of guests could occupy the property, which overlooked Pleasant Bay and sat on three hundred acres of land. The beachfront location was only the beginning, as Hotel Chatham also included a large horse stable, bowling alley, icehouse and bathhouses.

Hotel Chatham held weekly dances called social hops, bringing in some who could get a taste of the hotel without spending the night. The hotel's first season was booming, albeit short, as it closed not long after Labor Day. Still, this encouraged the ownership to enlarge the property to include one hundred guest rooms for the 1891 season. After reopening in June, more positive press came when the hotel hosted an event for then–Massachusetts governor William Russell and his staff that July. The success continued into the 1892 season, when, in August, the hotel and its one hundred guest rooms were full.

There were glimpses of success; however, the obstacles came hard and fast after the 1892 season. The Panic of 1893 closed numerous banks and ruined countless businesses, causing a depression that lasted into 1897. The ripple effect of this panic spelled the beginning of the end for the secluded luxury resort. Business suffered greatly, as people held on to what little money they had. This, coupled with the relative difficulty accessing the hotel, caused its demise.

The spot at the Eastward Ho! Golf Course where Hotel Chatham once stood. *Courtesy of Christopher Setterlund.*

In June 1894, the first reports of the hotel being up for sale came to light. The ownership had never turned a profit, despite some early success, and they shut down the resort after the 1894 season. Despite the bleak outlook, this was not an immediate end for the resort. In April 1895, the $150,000 property was purchased by Marcellus Eldredge for $16,000, as he had the intention of reopening for the 1895 season. This was not to be. Eldredge decided to move much of the purchased furniture to his other venture, the Dill House, which opened that same summer near the present-day intersection of Main Street and Shore Road in Chatham.

After Eldredge's death in 1898, his properties, including Hotel Chatham, were sold to Samuel Nickerson in 1900. The property sat in limbo, with a stock market crash of 1907 putting a damper on any plans for reopening. The hotel property was sold again to H.E. Austerland in 1909, and it was sold again to Robert Sanderson in 1910. Sanderson had the intention of renovating the resort and selling off the rest of the land in plots. This also did not happen. Late in 1910, the demolition of Hotel Chatham finally took place. It was remembered as a flash in the pan that spent more time shuttered in limbo than in business. Ironically, in 1912, funds were raised to improve the road that led to the former hotel property, as automobiles were coming into prominence. The remote location and several financial crises had doomed the first attempt to open a luxury resort on Cape Cod.

The second attempt came in 1914 with the opening of Chatham Bars Inn, which is still open more than a century later. The Hotel Chatham property gained new life in 1922, when it became the home of the Eastward Ho Country Club. For reference, the fourth-hole fairway of the present-day golf course was the spot where the ambitious luxury resort once stood in the first attempt to create a summer destination on Cape Cod.

HOTEL ENGLEWOOD

ADDRESS: MASSACHUSETTS AVENUE, WEST YARMOUTH
YEARS ACTIVE: 1902–1962

The body of water known as Lewis Bay on the central southern coast of Cape Cod has nearly seven miles of shoreline, mostly pristine beaches with incredible views. A few lucky individuals have the resources necessary to own property along this chunk of land, which makes running any sort of lodging business in the same area a smart and lucrative endeavor. One of the original waterfront hotels to pop up along Lewis Bay came around during the turn of the twentieth century. It was called Hotel Englewood, and for nearly sixty years, it gave travelers the true definition of a room with a view.

The idea for a hotel on the water in West Yarmouth was the brainchild of Philias T. Morin and his partner. The land that had once been the site of a saltworks held a pristine view of the calm waters of Lewis Bay. Morin, who had previously been a chef at a Boston hotel, lived steps away from the proposed site on Berry Avenue. He came to Yarmouth in 1901 to begin work on the twenty-five-room hotel. The building itself was constructed by George Eldridge, with a large portion of the money being fronted by people from Brockton who eventually become known as the Englewood Beach Land Company.

Stormy weather slowed the construction of the hotel; however, it was ready to be unveiled to the public the following summer. Opening night for the new hotel was June 17, 1902, and it was a huge success. It was highlighted by a group of two hundred people coming down to West Yarmouth from Brockton for the occasion. With six cottages already built next to the hotel, along with its own eponymously named beach, there was a feeling that Hotel

A postcard of the Englewood Hotel. *Courtesy of the Boston Public Library.*

Englewood would become a staple for travelers to Cape Cod for years to come. The fledgling hotel remained open between June and Labor Day, though the grounds were active during the late winter of 1903, with several new cottages being built around the main building.

The second season proved to be even more successful than the first, with Englewood being routinely overflowing with guests. In these early days, with automobiles still at a premium, stays at Englewood were much longer. Guests would arrive via railroad from Brockton, Boston, Providence and beyond and stay for several weeks at a time; sometimes, they would even stay for an entire summer before hopping back on the train. Guests could enjoy relaxing at the nearby beach of the same name or stay active with fishing, sailing, tennis and nearby golf. It was during this time that Morin leased the property from the Englewood Beach Land Company on his own. In December 1909, Hotel Englewood dodged a bullet when a cottage owned by Erastus Moulton, situated just behind it, burned to the ground. The fire was contained with no damage to other property, yet it was an ominous sign for the future of the hotel.

Two more cottages were added to the property in 1911. The largest change for Hotel Englewood came on December 19, 1912, when Philias Morin purchased the property outright from the Englewood Beach Land Company for a reportedly reasonable sum of $10,000 ($269,000 in 2021). The impact of this purchase was nearly immediate, as Morin added a new kitchen, several new cottages next to the hotel and brand-new electric lighting the following spring. Along with the new kitchen, Morin began raising chickens on the property and growing a vegetable garden to make the food served at Englewood as fresh as possible. The staff in the kitchen could even whip up broiled lobster or planked steaks on short notice. Morin promoted this fact in the local newspapers and the *Automobile Blue Book*. The popularity of the hotel could not be denied—so much so that Morin began keeping it open until the end of September in 1914.

Two new cottages and more improvements came to the Hotel Englewood in 1916, and its popularity only grew as automobiles became easier to come by. P.T. Morin was not one to rest on his laurels, so he put together an ambitious expansion project for the hotel in 1930. A seventy-two-by-thirty-seven-foot addition was built with fourteen new rooms at a cost of $20,000 ($313,000 in 2021). The expansion also included a large first-floor lounge and a larger front porch to give guests an even better view of Lewis Bay. The cuisine was also expanded, with Morin implementing seven-course meals for guests at breakfast, lunch and dinner. The new improvements were officially unveiled in May 1931, and a new wharf, which stretched out into Lewis Bay from Englewood Beach, was constructed around the same time.

Times began changing at Hotel Englewood in 1945. It was at this time that P.T. Morin, then in his early seventies, relinquished control of his beloved hotel to his three children: his sons, Francis and Hobart, and his daughter, Pauline. The children kept the hotel running strong through the remainder of the 1940s; however, a new development changed the dynamics of the establishment. The Mid-Cape Highway, constructed in 1954, made traveling by automobile far easier. This meant that stays at Hotel Englewood and other local lodging spots were shorter. Gone were the days of taking the train into town at the beginning of the summer and leaving around Labor Day.

In June 1960, the Morin Family sold their iconic hotel to John Kelley, who had some hotel experience through running the Nantasket House in Hull. The Morins helped Kelley and his son Francis become acclimated to daily life at Englewood; however, after fifty-eight years, their time at the hotel was over. Kelley had big plans for Hotel Englewood, including opening earlier in the spring, staying open until later in the fall, adding a swimming pool and putting green, creating a proper cocktail lounge and opening the dining area up as a restaurant to the public. In all, $400,000 ($3.5 million in 2021) was spent on improvements to the property, which had increased to include seventy-five rooms by this time. It seemed as though Hotel Englewood's next chapter would be even greater than its first.

The Inn at Lewis Bay, a former cottage of the Englewood Hotel. *Courtesy of Christopher Setterlund.*

But tragically, after only one full season of running the business, the end came for the hotel. On January 10, 1962, a fire broke out on the property in sixteen-degree weather, with strong winds fanning the flames. Despite seven local fire departments converging to put the fire out, it was not to be. The wildly popular Hotel Englewood was completely destroyed. It remained a dormant shell for two years before plans for rebuilding began to surface. In February 1964, Francis Kelley went before the town to get a permit to rebuild, and it was approved. By the end of 1964, a new establishment, the Englewood Motor Inn, was built on the property. However, it was not the same, and in 1985, the property was converted into condominiums and townhouses.

Though the Hotel Englewood may only be a distant memory, for those who wish to lay their eyes on a piece of its history, they only need to make a stop at the Inn at Lewis Bay. Located next to the former site of the hotel on Maine Avenue, the Inn at Lewis Bay resides in a former cottage of the famed Hotel Englewood. Photographs of the hotel adorn the walls inside, and this is a perfect way to get a taste of what it was like when Lewis Bay was home to one of Cape Cod's finest resort hotels.

HYANNIS INN

ADDRESS: 209 MAIN STREET, HYANNIS
YEARS ACTIVE: 1912–1968

In the early twentieth century, Cape Cod was becoming established as a summer getaway. There was also a growing number of people who chose to visit the Cape in the off-season. Seasonal lodging options were numerous, but year-round choices were far rarer. One location that was in need of a year-round hotel was the flourishing hub of Cape Cod Hyannis. The east end of Hyannis's Main Street was an up-and-coming business center around the turn of the twentieth century.

The person who brought year-round lodging to the east end of Hyannis was William E. Cox. Born in Boston, Cox came to Cape Cod in 1909. In 1911, he took over a restaurant in Hyannis that was previously owned by Charles Baker, next door to Louis Arenovski's popular American Clothing House, which was located near the downtown railroad depot. After running the restaurant for several months, a new opportunity opened up for Cox at the east end of Main Street. The building located at 209 Main Street, originally built in 1865, had been home to several different businesses before William Cox purchased it. The Daniel Crowell Store and residence, the Wyman House, the First National Bank and the Able D. Makepeace Building were all previous incarnations of 209 Main Street. In April 1912, Cox bought the building from Makepeace, who had owned it since May 1901.

The building was reopened as a hotel under the name Hyannis Inn in June 1912. It was painted white, with a brand-new sign hung from one of the majestic elm trees in front of the property. Cox added a piazza that fall

The Hyannis Inn. *Courtesy of the Sturgis Library.*

to help entice locals and visitors to give his new hotel a try. A year later, extensive improvements were made to Hyannis Inn, including the conversion of the piazza into a sunroom, the addition of ten rooms to the rear of the building and the construction of a new three-story addition that added eighteen rooms to the property. Mere months later, in January 1914, a large fire, which began in the kitchen, destroyed much of the rear of the building at a loss of $4,000 ($104,000 in 2021). Not only did the Hyannis Inn recover, it thrived. In November 1914, Cox had a laundry building erected that also included staff housing. During his tenure, there was a constant stream of improvements to the year-round hotel, which was capped with a pair of expansions. In March 1921, William Cox purchased the land behind the hotel, which was then owned by L.P. Wilson, and in June 1922, he purchased the land next to the hotel that was then owned by Mary Cash.

Cox sold the Hyannis Inn to James Goss and Paul Wadleigh for $100,000 ($1.47 million in 2021) in February 1926, as he was looking forward to retirement. Henry Haugh purchased the hotel not long after from Goss and Wadleigh while William Cox enjoyed a brief retirement. He came out of retirement in 1932, after a stint in Eastham in the poultry business, to open Bill Cox's Sea Grille on Bay View Street in West Yarmouth.

Haugh continued the trend of constant improvements at the inn, as he had it refurnished with gray wicker and dark-blue draperies as well as running water in each room. He also continued the tradition of having banquets in the dining hall for groups like the Cape Cod Chamber of Commerce, the Rotary Club, local firefighters and more. The property was a continued success throughout the 1930s and into the 1940s.

A pair of fires in August 1945 destroyed the kitchen and seemed to hamper Haugh's desire to continue at the hotel. The Hyannis Inn changed hands again in May 1946, when John and James Pendergast bought it. Henry Haugh moved out to Webster, Massachusetts, where he died that October. John Pendergast was the postmaster in Centerville, and while James was a no novice to the hotel business, he went to Boston University to learn as much as he could alongside another future Cape Cod hotel legend, Bob Stone of the Lighthouse Inn of West Dennis. James oversaw most of the management duties of the Hyannis Inn.

In June 1954, James purchased the Smith house on Main Street, just a half mile from the hotel. This became a very important purchase. The following year, the house was torn down to make way for another new hotel, which was initially called the Hyannis Motor Lodge and then the Hyannis Inn Motel. Later on, he built the Anchor-In Hotel on the corner of South Street and Lewis Bay Road. John Pendergast sold his interest in Hyannis Inn in 1956, when he also retired as postmaster.

As the 1960s arrived, Hyannis's Main Street became a more crowded place for businesses and hotels in general. Not only was there a $250,000 ($2 million in 2021) hotel called the Country Squire built directly across the street from the Hyannis Inn in 1965, but James Pendergast also constructed the East Ender Motor Lodge as a companion to Hyannis Inn on the same plot of land.

The Hyannis Inn came to an end in March 1968, when James Pendergast sold it to Joseph Piekutowski and it became known as Ye Bayberry Inne. That chapter was brief, however, and in 1969, a more successful chapter began when it became the Velvet Hammer Inn—later just the Velvet Hammer. Owned by Leonard Healy, it was seen as a "Top 40" club. The complex also included the Backside Saloon at its rear entrance and the Red Door establishment, which was located between the other two. The property saw success of varying degrees until 1982, when Velvet Hammer closed as it was prepared to be sold at auction. The Backside Saloon lasted into the mid-1990s as a separate entity. The former Hyannis Inn was repurposed as a retail space and apartment complex. James Pendergast's Hyannis Inn Motel and Anchor-In Hotel were still open in Hyannis as of 2021.

LAND'S END INN

ADDRESS: 22 COMMERCIAL STREET, PROVINCETOWN
YEARS ACTIVE: 1938–PRESENT

At the tip of Cape Cod, Provincetown has always had one foot in the present and the other locked in its rich history as a fishing village. One can walk Commercial Street or Bradford Street and find fine art galleries and world-class restaurants mixed with homes from the nineteenth century. Combined with striking views of the ocean, it is no wonder that visitors and locals flock to Provincetown. Perhaps no spot combines all of what makes this town special better than the Land's End Inn. For nearly a century, it has provided more than just a place to sleep—it has provided a place to make lasting memories. The inn began as a summer home and transitioned over time to become one of the most iconic resort hotels on the Cape.

The present-day Land's End Inn sits atop what was originally known simply as Gull Hill at the west end of Commercial Street. The hill, its surrounding pastures and waterfront land were all first owned by Captain Jonathan Nickerson. A third-generation sea captain, Nickerson helped form the Union Wharf Company in 1831 and build the Union Wharf in 1833, near present day 99–101 Commercial Street. After Nickerson's death in 1871, the property remained in limbo for decades. It was purchased by Charles Lothrop Higgins in September 1903. Higgins was a Provincetown native, a direct descendant of Pilgrim Peregrine White on his mother's side. In 1904, Higgins had a summer home built on Gull Hill; it was set unusually far back from the road, making it an arduous journey from the road up the hill to the home. The twenty-four-room home became known as the Higgins Bungalow, after the nonconformist and world traveler.

Land's End Inn. *Courtesy of Christopher Setterlund.*

The main body of the home was built on stilts, raising it higher than the surrounding land, and thanks to the ocean breeze, this gave it a sort of primitive air conditioning. The porches wrapped completely around the outside of the house, and a large fireplace and stained-glass nouveau chandelier enhanced the home's interior. Higgins's world traveling allowed him to fill his home with Chinese carvings and curios about which friends and visitors would rave. Perhaps the most unique feature of the home was the tower that held Higgins's private library. It had an octagonal shape and stained-glass windows, and it became a centerpiece of the estate's second chapter.

To complete Higgins's perfect vision, in 1909, he purchased a large steeped-roof house that blocked his full view of the water and had it moved down the street, where it became a candy store. Though the Higgins Bungalow was considered a private summer home, with Charles spending the winters on Boylston Street in Boston, the home hosted some functions and entertainment, such as a Shakespearean recital in August 1913. Usually, there was a small entrance fee of ten cents for his "at-home" receptions. In his later years, Higgins grew ill, and he passed away at the young age of sixty-three on March 23, 1926. His sole family member was a brother in Indiana, Elmer, who inherited the entirety of Charles's estate.

Elmer Higgins did not hold on to the Bungalow for long, and he ended up selling it to Miss Irene Buckler from Providence, Rhode Island. Buckler also used the bungalow as a summer retreat; however, she also began renting out rooms usually to friends from different parts of the Northeast. After a couple of seasons of using the home as a summer home and boardinghouse, Buckler opened the property up as a tearoom and function hall. The Higgins Bungalow was renamed the Land's End Tea House and had its grand opening on June 25, 1932.

After several successful summers at the fledgling teahouse, in 1938, Irene Buckler brought her brother Ernest Buckler aboard. It was at this time that the five-acre property became known as the Land's End Inn. Seemingly cut from a similar cloth as Charles Higgins, Ernest Buckler amassed artifacts from traveling abroad, many of which still decorate the interior of the inn today. One of the first changes the Buckler family made was the addition of ground-level rooms to the new inn. The sand that was removed to build the rooms was redistributed around the property to create flat areas where they grew grass and gardens. The Bucklers held on to the Land's End Inn until 1956, when it was sold to Jules Wade and his brother Norman Lague. This new ownership added a heating system, although the property had still not been winterized. Wade also helped immortalize Irene Buckler by donating a large collection of her books to the Provincetown Library in 1958. Wade and Lague were known to throw parties centered on a grand piano in the living room. However, in their last few years of owning the inn, business waned, partially due to the illness of one of their brothers.

In 1972, the property was sold, this time, to a man who altered Land's End Inn's trajectory more than any other. David Schoolman had been working with juvenile delinquents with a degree in clinical psychology before coming to Provincetown in 1971. Paying $139,000 ($898,000 in 2021) for what was basically seen as a dead business, Schoolman poured his heart and soul into Land's End. The new owner greatly expanded the building, capping it off with the Bay Tower in 1993. He made sure the hotel was properly winterized and properly plumbed, and he slowly but surely redecorated and reorganized it. Throughout the 1970s and into the 1980s, Schoolman added Art Nouveau treasures and the veranda to the inn. He made each room his own artistic interpretation, ranging from Art Deco and English country to casual Florida and more.

By the mid-1990s, Land's End Inn had become a legendary property, thanks, in great part, to David Schoolman. It even had a strong role in the 1995 comedy *Lie Down with Dogs*. Schoolman's death in 1995 at the age of fifty-one left a huge void in the hotel, and it fell into the hands of his David Adam Schoolman Trust. The inn began to fall into disrepair until Michael MacIntyre and Bob Anderson bought it in 2001 in the hopes of preserving the Provincetown landmark. They added air conditioning and television (by request of actress Kathleen Turner) and rehabilitated the once-proud gardens. After a decade of restoring the inn and enjoying great success, MacIntyre and Anderson sold Land's End in December 2012 to Stan and Eva Sikorski, who have continued the high level of quality the inn's countless visitors have come to expect.

Today Land's End Inn is a beautiful icon of Provincetown. It has eighteen unique rooms surrounded by scenery that most would pay double for. It is a destination in a town filled with destinations. David Schoolman summed up this Provincetown wonder perfectly in a 1993 interview: "I like to think of Land's End as an excellent bouillabaisse, everything goes together wonderfully."

LIGHTHOUSE INN

ADDRESS: 1 LIGHTHOUSE INN ROAD, WEST DENNIS
YEARS ACTIVE: 1938–PRESENT

The peninsula of Cape Cod is full of historical sites. There are a few rare spots on the Cape that are historic twice over. Such is the case in West Dennis, where a scenic seaside piece of property has a long, lustrous story.

The Lighthouse Inn, situated on Nantucket Sound, celebrated its eightieth anniversary in June 2018. However, the history associated with the site goes back almost another century. In order to aide in navigation for the increasing number of vessels traveling in the area during the mid-nineteenth century, Congress appropriated $4,000 in 1850 ($134,000 in 2021) to go toward the building of a lighthouse near the mouth of Bass River. It would take five years before the project was completed. On April 30, 1855, Bass River Lighthouse was lit for the first time. It was different from the typical lighthouse, as it consisted of a lantern mounted to the roof of a two-story home.

The construction of Stage Harbor Lighthouse in Chatham in 1880, only ten miles east, had lessened the need for the Bass River Light. The Cape Cod Canal helped ease vessel traffic along the south coast as well in 1914. This spelled the end of Bass River Light; it was dimmed on June 15, 1914, with the canal officially opening on July 29 that same year. The deactivated lighthouse property was sold and used as a summer home by Harry Noyes, who expanded the home and added other buildings to the property. After his death in 1933, the home was left vacant for five years; it wasn't until the property became occupied again that the second chapter of its history began.

The Lighthouse Inn. *Courtesy of Christopher Setterlund.*

In 1938, Massachusetts state senator Everett Stone and his wife, Gladys, purchased the property for $22,000 ($408,000 in 2021). Everett's initial intention was to develop the property and resell it. However, the paperwork was passed too late for any work to be done that year, so in order to help pay the mortgage, the Stones took in overnight guests. Ironically, many of those guests asked to return the following year, which changed the Stones' minds. Rather than resell the land, the Stones rechristened it the Lighthouse Inn.

In addition to the lodging accommodations, with room for up to 140 people, the nine-acre property included a restaurant inside the inn that was run by Everett and Gladys's son Bob. The dining area of the inn was eventually named the Waterfront Restaurant, and it became very popular for its cuisine, including steak and lobster, as well as its entertainment. From the 1950s to the 1980s, Bob and his wife, Mary, provided some of the best entertainment on Cape Cod. Their daughter Barbara Stone Amidon participated in some of the entertainment when she was young.

Amidon said:

> *In the 50's, 60's, 70's, and 80's, we had sing-alongs with various artists, dances, including beachcomber balls, where everyone came in costume;*

> *crazy hat parties, where people made hats from old menus, placemats and various other materials. There was ballroom dancing with a couple who taught at the old Belmont Hotel and who would come once a week or every other week to the Lighthouse. During the 60's, we published a weekly newspaper for the guests, and the entertainment schedule included: "Piano with Gladys," "Sing with Betty and Gladys," "Cape Cod Slides," "Man with a Thousand Songs," "Songs by the Inn-tertainers"* [waiters who would put on a show], *and, of course, Bingo, which I called for a number of years as a teenager, and my brothers took over after me.*

Though the Stones and their five children were active participants in the entertainment, the ace in the hole was noted pianist Ken Manzer. For decades, the talented musician was showcased at Lighthouse Inn; he also moved along when the Stones opened a pair of other ventures, Bishop's Terrace in Harwich and Deacon's Perch in Yarmouth Port.

In 1989, the inn went full circle. On August 7, 1989, Bass River Light, which had been deactivated for seventy-five years, was relit. Renamed West Dennis Light, it is now used as an active navigational aide during the summer. Though the inn has been rocked by hurricanes in the past due to its proximity to the ocean, including during Hurricane Bob in 1991, the Lighthouse Inn and the Stone family are still going strong.

Even after more than eight decades of service, the establishment is still hugely popular, with its sixty-one rooms and cottages routinely filled. It offers scenic views in addition to the Waterfront Restaurant, tennis, a heated pool and a private beach, just in case West Dennis Beach is too far of a walk. There are also tours available of the privately owned and operated lighthouse.

Although Bob and Mary have passed on, the inn remains in the family. All five of their children, Betty Anne, Deborah, Barbara, Jonathan and Greg, have worked there at some point, and as of 2021, the property was still managed by Greg and his wife, Patricia. It is a piece of living history that is still thriving in its third generation of Stone family management.

OCEAN EDGE RESORT AND GOLF CLUB

ADDRESS: 2907 ROUTE 6A, BREWSTER
YEARS ACTIVE: 1981–PRESENT

The property that is known today as the Ocean Edge Resort began its life as part of a much larger tract of land owned by one of the most prominent families in Cape Cod history: the Nickerson family.

Samuel Nickerson was born in Chatham in 1830, yet he traveled far and wide before returning to Cape Cod. By the age of seventeen, Samuel had found his way to Apalachicola, Florida, where he worked with his brother, Sparrow, at his general store. He had varied success until he married Mathilda Pinkham Crosby in 1858. Her family had been involved in the wholesale liquor business. This connection led Samuel to Chicago, where, after establishing his own liquor company, he found his way into finance. Nickerson became the vice-president of Chicago's First National Bank in 1863, and he became its president in 1867. His fortune, at one point, was estimated at $5 million ($137.6 million in 2021), according to newspaper articles from 1887.

In the late-1880s, Samuel purchased a large tract of land in Brewster that overlooked Cape Cod Bay; there, he built a summer home for his family. The three-story home was erected in 1890 on a forty-eight-acre parcel of land, and it was called Fieldstone Hall. Much of the remainder of the property was used as a private game reserve for the Nickersons and their guests.

In May 1906, Fieldstone Hall burned to the ground. Though he was pulled to safety, Samuel's health never recovered, and he died only two weeks later. Addie Nickerson, the widow of Samuel's son Roland, immediately began planning to rebuild Fieldstone Hall alongside Samuel's

The Nickerson Mansion at Ocean Edge. *Courtesy of Christopher Setterlund.*

son Samuel Jr. Samuel Jr. suggested fireproof concrete and stucco as the materials for the larger mansion. It was finished in 1912, standing on the footprint of the original.

In 1934, Addie Nickerson donated approximately 1,727 acres of land to the state. The area south of Route 6A, formerly the Nickerson private game reserve, was rechristened Nickerson State Park. It was the first state park in Massachusetts. After Addie passed away in July 1940, Fieldstone Hall was put up for sale. It sat on the market until January 1945, when it was purchased by the LaSalette Seminary Corporation, which also had properties in Attleboro, Massachusetts, and Enfield, New Hampshire. It was ready to be used as a seminary in April that year.

Though it was a religious seminary, LaSalette would routinely invite the public to the old Nickerson estate for clambakes on the beach. In the 1970s, LaSalette was in the news routinely. In 1973, it was put to the town that the property, then valued at over $1.2 million ($7.11 million in 2021), should be taxed, despite the fact that religious organizations are usually tax exempt. Financial difficulties caused the LaSalette order to put the property up for sale.

In May 1974, the property was sold to Frederick Walters and Martin Rich for $1.45 million ($7.69 million in 2021), and they began looking at alternative uses for the former seminary. Perhaps the strangest of these occurred in January 1975, when the Douglas Zeppelin Company appealed to the Town of Brewster to allow them to build zeppelins on the property of LaSalette. Later in 1975, Brewster selectmen tried to acquire state funding to buy the property, but the state could only offer half of what was being asked, and the plan quickly died. The property was later viewed as a potential alcohol detox center; however, nothing came from that either.

In August 1979, the first rumblings of a major change to the former Nickerson estate were made. The rumor was that LaSalette might be up for sale to be converted into a two-hundred- to four-hundred-room resort; though nothing was certain at the time. On September 10, 1979, the property was officially sold to the Corcoran, Mullins and Jennison (CMJ) Corporation, which owned the Sea Pines Condominiums a half mile away on Route 6A. The company initially planned to convert LaSalette into a luxury condominium complex. The name Ocean Edge was first mentioned in a newspaper article in December 1979. In trying to appease the town, the new owners adhered to a list of twenty-five conditions set forth by the Historic District Committee.

Work quickly began on the 130-unit condominium complex and resort in July 1980, once all of the conditions were understood. There had been more than two dozen condos built by the spring of 1981, and tennis courts, a swimming pool and a clubhouse had been built by that summer. In March 1982, advertisements began popping up in local newspapers, saying that the new two-bedroom, two-bathroom Ocean Edge condos were being sold for prices as low as $148,900 ($403,600 in 2021). In September 1982, the CMJ Corporation was given the green light to build ninety one-bedroom villas that were to be available for rent on the Ocean Edge property, thus opening up the area as a luxury resort. These villas would not be visible from Route 6A, a condition set on CMJ by the Town of Brewster.

An addition was built behind the Fieldstone Hall, which became the Ocean Grille dining facility; a liquor license was granted in August 1983. The golf course on the south side of Route 6A, first known as Brewster Golf Course, became known as the Ocean Edge Golf Course in 1984. The promised conference center, which was part of the initial genesis of the development of Ocean Edge, took longer to become reality, and it did not officially open inside Fieldstone Hall until June 2, 1986. It was worth the wait, as several influential companies, including Bank of Boston and Filene's, booked conferences there almost immediately. CMJ made sure to maintain the original charm of the historic mansion, leaving the chandeliers,

The Beach Bar at Ocean Edge. *Courtesy of Christopher Setterlund.*

mahogany-carved staircase and two impressive fireplaces, one of marble and one of sandstone.

The sprawling lawn in front of the former Fieldstone Hall, renamed the Nickerson Mansion, became a popular spot for elegant weddings. In later years, the Beach House Spa was added to further relaxation. Today, more than thirty years after first opening to both visitors who were just staying for a few nights and year-round residents alike, Ocean Edge Resort and Golf Club is going strong and racking up accolades. It was voted "Cape Cod's Best Resort" by *Boston Magazine* four years in a row, including in 2020. The Nickerson Mansion, specifically, had been regarded as one of the "Best Resorts in Massachusetts" by *Condé Nast Traveler*.

From its beginnings as the estate of the influential Nickerson family more than a century ago, all the way through to the current day, the beauty and charm of Ocean Edge has been undeniable. Whether you take a quick tour of the Nickerson Mansion, which is open to the public; go for a night's stay; play an eighteen-hole game of golf; attend a wedding; or move in permanently to the Villages at Ocean Edge, it is a safe bet you will enjoy your time there.

OLD YARMOUTH INN

ADDRESS: 223 ROUTE 6A, YARMOUTH PORT
YEARS ACTIVE: 1696–PRESENT

The history of the Old Yarmouth Inn goes back nearly to the beginning of the town of Yarmouth itself. The town was incorporated in 1639, and just over a half a century later, what became Old Yarmouth Inn first came into existence. Today, it is one of the most iconic and beloved restaurants on Cape Cod. However, this spot has been on a roller coaster ride, as is expected for any place that has existed for more than three centuries. Old Yarmouth Inn has played different roles and gone through many changes, yet it has always remained integral to the fabric of Cape society.

The property that is known today as the Old Yarmouth Inn dates all the way back to 1696. When it was first opened, the inn was used as a stage stop and wayside inn along the Old Kings Highway, which is known today as Route 6A. It was the end of the line for people who were traveling to Cape Cod from Boston.

The stage stop along the Old King's Highway began a historic chapter when it was bought by Charles Sears in 1830. Having previously been a deputy sheriff and postman, the portly but congenial Sears, along with his wife, Elizabeth, renamed the property the Sears Hotel. It became an immediate success as a hostelry, and it continued its legacy as a stage stop. Charles Sears was friendly and welcoming, which led to his hotel becoming extremely popular among those who visited from far and wide despite it having a no-alcohol policy in place. Sears added extra stagecoach departure times and routes in the late 1840s to accommodate not only visitors to his hotel but also local Cape Codders, naturally drawing more attention to his

Old Yarmouth Inn. *Courtesy of Christopher Setterlund.*

hotel. In October 1849, during his first trip to Cape Cod, author Henry David Thoreau made it a point to stop at the Sears Hotel, making him one of the many high-profile guests to stay there. Charles Sears maintained control of the hotel, despite getting involved in local politics in the early 1850s. He was being stretched thin, and eventually, he relinquished control of the inn to Charles Conant in 1854. However, Conant's tenure was short-lived, and Sears was soon back in charge. In August 1857, Sears again relinquished control, this time, to his son Charles Jr.

The inn's success continued, as the first summer under Charles Jr. saw the hotel filled, and its reputation for comfortable accommodations and good cheer only grew. However, the hotel business was not for Charles Sears Jr., and he sold the property to Ebenezer Hallett in November 1859. After nearly thirty years, the Sears family was no longer involved with the popular hotel. Though the inn continued to be a success during his tenure, Hallett had his eyes elsewhere. In March 1868, he took over the Pilgrim House in Provincetown, leaving the Sears Hotel to be sold at auction.

The Sears Hotel did not sit vacant for long; however, its days as a hotel came to an end for the foreseeable future. On September 5, 1868, Rufus E. Holmes of Worcester purchased the property for $3,000 ($55,200 in 2021). Holmes did extensive remodeling on the interior of the former hotel, which he used as a private residence while he ran a market in town. Though it remained a private summer home for years, the legacy of the Sears Hotel lingered. At one point in 1883, the local newspaper printed Holmes's Worcester address, urging Yarmouth residents to write him and ask him to allow his property to once again be run as a hotel. Any pleas that were sent fell on deaf ears for the remainder of the nineteenth century.

In October 1900, Holmes leased the former hotel, which became a boardinghouse while he remained in Worcester. After Holmes's death in January 1907, the property was passed down to his children, who held on to it until October 1921, when it was sold to Frank G. Phinney, and a new chapter began for the legendary former stage stop.

Phinney had also previously run the Barnstable Inn and was very familiar with the hotel business. By mid-November 1921, Phinney had remodeled the building and renamed it the Yarmouth Tavern. It was once again a full-fledged hotel, just as it had been under the Sears family. It was a seasonal establishment, remaining open from May to November. It had ten rooms for guests, some with private baths, and it prided itself on the exquisite home-cooked meals it served in its thirty-five-seat dining room. Phinney left Yarmouth Tavern for the Crosby House in 1928, with Ernest Sharpe taking over. All of the rooms were refurnished under Sharpe's brief tenure, which lasted less than a year. Bradford Powell became the owner of Yarmouth Tavern in May 1929. His major change to the establishment was making it a year-round business, with special low winter rates. These low rates were extended into April and May 1931, coinciding with major improvements to the property. The Yarmouth Tavern drew the admiration of actress Edith Barrett, the future wife of icon Vincent Price, as she stayed there several times during her engagements at the Cape Playhouse in 1932 and 1933.

After the 1935 season, Powell closed the Yarmouth Tavern and did not reopen it. In January 1936, the building became property of the Home Owners' Loan Corporation. Robert Powdrell of Wellfleet purchased Yarmouth Tavern in December 1939 with the intention of remodeling it and using it as an inn and as his family's residence. Those grand plans never materialized, and after a failed bid in 1940 to secure a liquor license for the tavern, it again became vacant. During World War II, the property served a greater purpose, as it became a home to servicemen who were stationed in Wellfleet. More than a decade of instability in ownership took its toll on the legacy of the Yarmouth Tavern. In August 1944, Nellie Barrington, who owned a pair of inns and another pair of boardinghouses around Boston, purchased the business and took her shot at running it as an inn.

Barrington used her previous lodging experience to begin to change Yarmouth Tavern into what it is today. She began by adding a new main dining room and opening it to the public on July 1, 1945. Nellie also purchased the neighboring Sears Arms estate, renaming it Boxwood Manor. The inn remained open year round, enticing guests with a 10 percent discount after Labor Day. The fireplaces and low ceilings left from the Colonial era became an extra source of charm and comfort for guests and diners alike. Barrington sold Yarmouth Tavern to Harold Peters in March 1948, while retaining Boxwood Manor. After some debate about renaming the inn Stage Coach Inn, a new name was settled on: Old Yarmouth Inn.

The name stuck, but the management did not. In May 1950, the business was again sold, this time, to former West Point chef Harry Rudelt and his wife, Kathryn. The couple were the most stable owners since the days of Charles Sears Sr. There was extensive remodeling during the tenure of the Rudelts, including the razing of a decaying old barn on the property in November 1961 to make way for more parking. For twenty years, Harry and Kathryn put their hearts and souls into restoring the property and its legacy. Their relationship with the town, their employees and their guests hearkened back to the cheery days of the Sears Hotel. The couple felt they had done all they could and sold the inn in 1970 to father and son James and Shane Peros.

Shane bought Boxwood Manor in 1972 and turned it into Old Yarmouth Manor, a guest house for the inn. He also took great interest in discovering the property's history. This led him to search high and low in the main building, where he discovered an old guest book from the 1860s, among other artifacts, in an unknown cupboard located near the fireplace in the bar room. In May 1990, after two decades of ownership, the Peroses sold Old Yarmouth Inn. By this point, the inn was known more for its cuisine and live music than its lodging, although that was still popular. The Red Room, Music Room and Main Dining Room, on their own, were sights to see before the food even arrived. During the 1990s, the restaurant and inn changed hands several times, but its popularity did not wane. Finally, Arpad Voros and Sheila Fitzgerald brought stability back to the inn at the end of the twentieth century.

Today, Old Yarmouth Inn is considered to be the epitome of class on Cape Cod. It combines modern dining with history that guests can reach out and touch. Although the lodging aspect of Old Yarmouth Inn officially ended in 2007, the experience there is still one of a kind. Sheila Fitzgerald continues to adapt to the changing times and has added a popular Sunday brunch buffet and prix fixe menu. After more than three centuries and countless changes, Old Yarmouth Inn, the former stagecoach stop, seems to show no signs of slowing down.

ORLEANS INN

ADDRESS: 3 OLD COUNTY ROAD, ORLEANS
YEARS ACTIVE: 1931–PRESENT

Orleans Inn began its existence as an integral part of Orleans's Snow family nearly 150 years ago. Overlooking Town Cove, it seemed to be a failure at first. It then went on to become one of the most well-known inns on Cape Cod due to its location and views, high-quality food and drink and its status as a haunted house.

The connection between the Snow family and Cape Cod, specifically Orleans, runs deep. The patriarch of the family in America, Nicholas Snow, arrived in Plymouth in 1624. He married Mayflower passenger Constance Hopkins, and the two moved to what was then known as the Nauset region on Cape Cod. Later, that region became the towns of Truro, Wellfleet, Eastham and Orleans, with Nicholas's descendant Isaac Snow helping incorporate and name Orleans in 1797.

Nearly a century after the town was born, another Snow, Aaron Snow II, began to work on what became the Orleans Inn. The fourteen-room building with a mansard roof was erected in 1875 on nine acres of prime waterfront land; it was the home for Snow, his wife, Mary, and their seven children. On the water, Snow built a wharf, which was the home of his fifty-five-ton schooner, the *Nettie M. Rogers*. Snow would travel along the shores of New England, gathering a cargo of timber, coal, grains, whale oil and more, and he would then sell these items at a general store he ran in the front room of the dwelling. It was renovated and enlarged several times during the following years and became known as Snow's Block. The general store was moved to the center of town in 1887 by Aaron's son William and his wife,

Annie. There, they were able to take advantage of the railroad line, which had made its way there. The store remains in operation today as Snow's Cape Cod. The railroad siphoned off business from Snow's original general store during the mid-1880s, rendering it uneconomical. This led some in town to later refer to Snow's Block as "Aaron's Folly."

After being in poor health for three years, Aaron Snow died on May 10, 1892. His wife, Mary, died three months later. Within a few years of his death, Snow's home had been sold twice, including once, in 1895, when it was sold at auction for only $1,000 ($31,100 in 2021). In 1896, a potential buyer from Winthrop was looking to turn the Snow estate into a hotel; however, nothing came from it. Finally, in 1901, William Doyle bought the property and began running it as a boardinghouse. Doyle kept the property until 1912, when he sold it to Edwin Ellis. Ellis continued to run it as a boardinghouse known as the Cove Inn before selling it to Mary Cushman in 1925. This was when the property got its now-familiar name.

Christened the Orleans Inn, it remained a boardinghouse for a few more years. In 1931, the inn was sold to Caroline Stearns, who had hotel management experience. She remodeled the property and added a new piazza that faced the cove. By the end of the new hotel's second summer season, in 1933, business had tripled from the year before, thanks to the extensive remodeling as well as the high-quality food that was being served to guests. In 1936, Stearns swapped the ownership of the inn with George Linnell, who owned the neighboring Dr. Wilson estate. Linnell only retained the Orleans Inn for two seasons before selling it to George Carlson. The numerous ownership changes during the beginning of the twentieth century made it difficult for the establishment to gain any momentum.

The Orleans Inn gained a sense of traction during the tenure of its next owner, Bruno Burkhardt. After purchasing the inn from Carlson in 1943, Burkhardt added two new wings to the building. A new invention called television first reached the Outer Cape via the Orleans Inn in 1948. The seasonal hotel became a year-round establishment with a new focus on dining. It then had more than one spot to enjoy food and drink, including the Aft Deck Dining Room, the Brunella Room and Lounge and the Below Deck Bar. In 1957, that focus on dining shifted even further with the sale of the property to restaurateurs Nicholas Vroundgos and Agamemnon Commatas. The new owners drastically changed the Orleans Inn, converting it into a seafood restaurant. The interior was altered to include fish net motifs at the entrance, a lobster pool in the upstairs entrance hall and a newly named Sunset Patio for warmer days. The new owners did maintain the lodging aspect of the property, though it was seen as secondary to the eating establishment.

The Orleans Inn drifted further from its roots as a boardinghouse with its sale in 1963 to Ed Martin. Newspaper advertisements at the time rarely, if ever, mentioned rooms for rent at the property. In 1974, it was renamed the Orleans Inn of the Yankee Fishermen after being purchased by the then-owner of the Captain Linnell House Dennis Stamatos. Major changes were planned, yet again, with the restaurant having a maximum capacity of 250 and the twenty rooms upstairs being redone and made available for rent. Stamatos ran the establishment under an inn-holders license. However, he went bankrupt after two years, and the inn was sold again, eventually winding up in the hands of John and Dorothy Guenther, who maintained the new name of the historic property.

The inn began to deteriorate physically and in reputation as the 1980s drew to a close. Liquor violations put it on the town's radar, and financial difficulties and the need for an upgraded septic system shut the landmark down for several months. It was subsequently foreclosed on in May 1990, and it was closed and put up for auction. It appeared as though the Orleans Inn was history.

In November 1991, the Orleans Inn was resurrected by new owners Richard Papas, formerly of the Barley Neck Inn, and Matthew Sutphin. The pair reacquired a liquor license; performed all necessary repairs on the property, which had been dormant for many months; and reopened with a bang on March 23, 1992. By early 1996, the financial problems had crept back in, and once again, the Orleans Inn was in danger of being foreclosed on. This time, there was a movement in the town of Orleans to purchase the stately manor and turn it into an arts center. The inn's future was up in the air.

In August 1996, Edward and Laurie Maas came to the rescue, purchasing the Orleans Inn and beginning the arduous task of restoring stability to the establishment. The inn was reopened in May 1997, and for over twenty years, the Maases have presided over the most successful chapter in the property's nearly 150-year history.

As far as the property being a haunted house goes, Ed Maas has gone on record to identify three consistent ghost presences, most notably, Hannah, a young woman who was purportedly murdered in front of the inn during the 1920s. She is known to be seen walking or dancing naked in the inn's rooms. The hauntings gained more notoriety thanks to Maas's book *Ghost of the Orleans Inn*, as well as an episode of Syfy's *Ghosthunters*.

The Orleans Inn. *Courtesy of Christopher Setterlund.*

Beautifully renovated rooms, high-quality cuisine and the chance to see ghosts are all part of what gives the Orleans Inn and Restaurant its tremendous appeal today. From its beginning as "Aaron's Folly," to its chapter as the Yankee Fishermen, this wondrous icon of Orleans has weathered multiple storms and has come out as a living legend of Cape Cod.

THE PINES

ADDRESS: OCEAN VIEW AVENUE, COTUIT
YEARS ACTIVE: 1893–1958

The town of Barnstable is made up of seven unique villages: Barnstable, Centerville, Cotuit, Hyannis, Osterville, Marstons Mills and West Barnstable. Each one has popular attractions, pristine beaches and quaint shops. Located in the southeastern corner of Barnstable is the village of Cotuit, meaning "place of the council" in Wampanoag. The village was known as Cotuit Port until 1872, and it was around this time that Cotuit—and Cape Cod as a whole—began to be discovered as a popular summer destination. It was late in the nineteenth century that the first generation of resort hotels began popping up on the Cape. Overlooking Cotuit Bay, one such legend of Cape Cod lodging rose and welcomed countless guests for more than sixty years. It was called the Pines.

The story of the Pines began in 1808 with a homestead built by Samuel Dottridge on present-day Ocean View Avenue. Dottridge was a carpenter by trade who came to Brewster from London in 1804; he married Abigail Chase in 1808. When he decided to move his family from Brewster to Cotuit, the house was pulled by oxen, over the dirt roads the entire way. By 1837, Dottridge had built a barn, expanded his three-room home to a five-room home, owned forty-five acres of land and ran 1,150 feet of saltworks at Bluff Point to the east. After Abigail's death in 1848, Dottridge left his homestead to his children and moved to Sandwich, where he lived until his death in 1854.

In 1891, Elizabeth Nickerson Morse, the granddaughter of Samuel Dottridge, opened a boardinghouse on the homestead. The following year,

Elizabeth and her husband, John Morse, bet on themselves and built a three-story building with thirty-three rooms on the Dottridge property. On June 17, 1893, the resort hotel known as the Pines, named for the vast pine trees of Cotuit, had its grand opening. Since the hotel was on the Dottridge family's property and was run by family, it was natural that Elizabeth and John would proclaim the Pines to be a family resort. This meant that there would be no alcohol and no gambling; however, it more than made up for those two things. First, the private beach that resided on Cotuit Bay was a big draw. The Pines also provided high-quality food and, eventually, an ice cream parlor, sailboats for rent and even rides to nearby freshwater ponds for guests.

The Morses thrilled guests with their Fourth of July festivities, including a clambake, a sawing match and boat races. The Pines was an immediate hit, and it allowed Elizabeth and John to take more calculated risks in running their establishment. It began in earnest at the turn of the twentieth century, with the couple enlarging the hotel as much as they could. It continued with the purchase of the retired sea captains' cottages that surrounded the Pines, effectively adding rooms to the hotel without building an addition. The family-friendly atmosphere of the resort, coupled with the classic seaport feel of Cotuit, made the Pines a repeat destination for visitors and garnered it regional and national attention. The summer season saw the rooms and cottages full much of the time.

Elizabeth Morse died in 1908, and John died in 1910; the hotel was then taken over by their daughter Nita, the great-granddaughter of Samuel Dottridge. One of her first acts as owner was to move the original Dottridge homestead back from Ocean View Avenue and use it as the laundry building for the Pines. In 1913, Nita married Calvin Crawford, and the two ran the hotel together, despite initially being reluctant and looking for a potential buyer.

In 1915, the Pines had a capacity of about fifty people, and the weekly rates were reasonable. A guest could rent a room for $13 a week ($336 in 2021); this included the room and three meals a day and was known as the "American Plan." Mr. and Mrs. Crawford oversaw a highly successful period for the Pines, and as the 1910s entered the 1920s, their family-friendly resort was not affected by Prohibition. In 1920, Crawford purchased the neighboring home of the late insurance mogul Alexander Adams; it was renovated and became the Pine Tree Tea Room. This became another family attraction, serving ice cream and sodas. In the 1940s, it became known as Sign of the Pine Tree. In 1936, Calvin Crawford bought the old

Cotuit Firehouse at auction and had it moved to the property, renaming it the Lundquist Cottage.

Calvin Crawford, in addition to his duties at the Pines, became a much more prominent member of Cape Cod as time went on. During the 1920s, he frequented town meetings; this advanced to him becoming elected president of Massachusetts Hotel Association. His highest local recognition came when he was elected as president of the Cape Cod Chamber of Commerce in 1947, succeeding Donald Trayser. Despite the increasing outside responsibilities, Crawford never lost sight of his commitments to the Pines. He added on to the Pines by purchasing a twenty-four-room mansion known as Evergreen located near the resort shortly after World War II.

However, the vacation habits of Americans were changing as the 1950s approached. Gone were the days of spending weeks or even an entire summer at a hotel or resort; they were replaced with shorter stays. The legacy and longevity of the Pines helped it stay afloat for several years during the changing times, and it reached its sixtieth anniversary in June 1953. The occasion was marked with a huge celebration that included speeches, a tour of the resort grounds and a luncheon.

Dottridge Homestead, which became the laundry room of the Pines. *Courtesy of Christopher Setterlund.*

In 1958, the Crawfords decided that it was time to drop the curtain on the Pines, making its sixty-fifth season in business its last. The announcement was made prior to the hotel opening in June so that the final season could be a celebratory last hurrah for the untold number of guests who had frequented the Pines through the decades. Calvin and Nita Crawford put most of the items on the property up for sale at auction once the Pines officially closed its doors in September 1958. These items included paintings, boats, pool tables, pianos and office equipment. After forty-five years of ownership, the Crawfords enjoyed a quiet retirement, including a celebratory dinner shortly after the Pines closed at another iconic Cape Cod hotel, the Lighthouse Inn.

Piece by piece, the cottages and the resort hotel itself were sold or dismantled after the Pines closed. The only remnant of those days that is still accessible to the public is, ironically, the spot that started it all. The home of Samuel Dottridge, which was inherited by his great-granddaughter Nita Crawford, was repurposed as the home of the Historical Society of Santuit and Cotuit. It stands stoically on Main Street at the front end of the majestic property that Dottridge had once owned and that had, for sixty-five years, been home to one of the finest resort hotels in Cape Cod's history.

POPPONESSET INN

ADDRESS: 252 SHORE DRIVE, MASHPEE
YEARS ACTIVE: 1941–PRESENT

In the town of Mashpee lies an area that is widely considered to be at the top of the list for weddings on Cape Cod. Located among the luxury that is New Seabury is the Popponesset Inn. For nearly seventy years, this establishment has been thrilling diners, travelers and wedding guests alike. Though its history as a luxury recreation area is more recent, Popponesset has been attracting throngs of visitors for much longer.

The beginnings of Popponesset, possibly named for a Wampanoag sachem of the mid-seventeenth century, occurred just after World War I. Rhode Island industrialist Malcolm G. Chace had been visiting his grandfather's home in Falmouth's village of Wianno in Cape Cod since he was a boy. In 1929, Chace, along with the rest of his Nantucket Sound Associates group, bought much of the land along Mashpee's south shore, which was then owned by the Greater Cotuit Shore Company. Chace was also the owner of Great Island in West Yarmouth, which he had turned into a summer community for his family in the mid-1920s.

Though Popponesset was mostly owned by Chace's organization, the 1930s saw the property become a summer tourist getaway. In 1933, Norma Armstrong, a nurse by trade, leased four thousand acres of land on the six-mile Popponesset Beach, where she had opened a tourist camp and ran a small general store. For several years during the summer, countless tents, trailers and cabins rose up along the beach as more than six thousand travelers made it their temporary home. The area became affectionately known as "Tent City." Coming from as far away as Texas, the people who

The entrance to Popponesset Inn. *Courtesy of Kent Earle.*

stayed at Armstrong's camp could afford rooms in local hotels but preferred to stay in the relative seclusion and obscurity of Popponesset.

In 1937, larger, permanent homes began to spring up on nearby Daniels Island, while some of Armstrong's campers purchased small plots of land from Roy Wilson in an area known today as Wilson's Grove. Though Armstrong's Tent City was ended after the 1939 season, it was clear that Popponesset's popularity was only going to climb.

In 1940, Popponesset became a proper resort destination. Under the management of Joseph Sonntag, sixteen cottages were built in time for the summer. The new summer resort was to be for those of moderate financial means, a difference from Norma Armstrong's tourist camp. However, the property kept its relative obscurity and isolation from the rest of the Cape, giving it a mixture of luxury and rural life for travelers. In addition to the cottages, two tennis courts, a shuffleboard court and a forty-by-eighty-foot open-air pavilion were built along the pristine Popponesset Beach. The property also had an inn that was modeled after ancient California mission buildings. At first, ten rooms were ready to be rented, with fifteen more becoming ready in 1941. Every room had a private exit to the beach. The Popponesset Inn was born.

The resort area continued to grow around the inn. By the end of the 1941 season, the property included twenty-eight beach houses and forty-one summer homes. During World War II, a firing range was built that brought hundreds of soldiers from Camp Edwards to Popponesset. After the war ended, a few of the soldier housing units were turned into summer homes. Edna Harris, the manager of the Coonamessett Inn in Falmouth, took over the management of the entire Popponesset resort in 1947, and she placed her daughter Hilda Coppage in charge of the inn. It was during this time that a beach pavilion was built with cabanas. Coppage ran many banquet dinners at the inn, much like she had at Coonamessett. There was also a regular square dance program that was held for several years at the Deck at Popponesset.

Despite the Popponesset property being seen as a luxury resort for members, Hilda Coppage would occasionally open the inn and restaurant to the public during the 1950s. Coppage became a star of the property with her rapid-fire wit with newspapers during the late 1950s, and many compared her to Phyllis Diller. Around this time, Popponesset got a new neighbor. In 1961, plans were unveiled for a sprawling luxury village called New Seabury; it was to be located on nearly 2,700 acres of land next to Popponesset. Malcolm Chace's sons Malcolm Jr. and Arnold established the new community, which opened in 1964 with ninety-one homes. A golf course and clubhouse were opened in 1965. A beach club was also built on the Popponesset Spit, a long stretch of barrier beach that protects Popponesset Bay. New Seabury gave up on the beach club on the spit, and in 1973, it built a new club close to Popponesset Inn. Also during the early 1970s, William Henry took over the management of Popponesset, as he had returned to Cape Cod from Boston to pursue a career in real estate.

The Popponesset Inn's ascension to a premier wedding venue began with a change in management in 1988. Bill and Linda Zammer, after moving permanently to Mashpee, took a leap of faith and took over management of the property. It was the Zammers who decided to erect a tent on the beach to entice couples to have their weddings there. The foray into hotel and restaurant management proved to be such a success that the Zammers bought the Flying Bridge Restaurant and Coonamessett Inn, both in Falmouth, in the forthcoming years.

In 1998, the entire 1,500 acres of New Seabury, including the Popponesset Inn, was purchased by Carl Icahn, an international financier with American Real Estate Partners (now Icahn Enterprises). This was the first time the property had not been owned by the Chace family since its opening. Icahn's company still owned the property as of 2020.

Fittingly, today, the Popponesset Inn, closing in on eighty years of existence, is more in touch with its roots than it has ever been before. The large wedding tent on the beach hearkens back to the days when Norma Armstrong oversaw the summer tourist camp known as Tent City. It is more than a world-class wedding destination, though it was voted Cape Cod's "best location" for a wedding by the readers of *Cape Cod LIFE Magazine* for eight consecutive years from 2012 to 2019. Popponesset is a resort and

Popponesset Inn and Beach from the air. *Courtesy of Kent Earle.*

restaurant as well, allowing for more of the general public to enjoy what it is all about. There are no bad views from the interior of the restaurant. The beach scenery outside is captured beautifully on the inside, with several hand-painted murals by Cape Cod artist Mindy Reasonover.

As far as the enduring appeal of Popponesset, it is summed up perfectly by Bob Higgins, the director of membership at the Club at New Seabury: "The secret to the inn is its location. You are literally on the beach, enjoying everything the Cape has to offer. Great food, drinks and entertainment with the backdrop of a beautiful private beach and views of Nantucket Sound."

PROVINCETOWN INN

ADDRESS: 1 COMMERCIAL STREET, PROVINCETOWN
YEARS ACTIVE: 1922–PRESENT

The Pilgrims and their journey to America is firmly entwined with the iconic Provincetown Inn. From the fact that it was originally developed by a descendant of the spiritual leader of the Pilgrims to its location being mere steps away from where the Mayflower first landed, this legendary hotel has remained a fixture in Provincetown for nearly a century. It was built when the town at the tip of the Cape was still predominantly a fishing village, and it still stands tall, as the twenty-first century has brought high class, fine art and modern chic to the town.

Provincetown native Joshua Paine, the creator of the inn, was a descendant of the spiritual leader of the Pilgrims Elder William Brewster through his mother, Martha Freeman Atwood. In 1921, the seeds for a Provincetown icon were first sown, although in far different location from where it is today. The beginnings of the Provincetown Inn are shrouded in mystery, as the dates of its completion and the function of the property differ between sources. According to the hotel's own website, the property saw the opening of a "new luxurious hotel" in Provincetown. However, the *Provincetown Advocate* and *Barnstable Patriot* newspaper archives and the late local historian Clive Driver put the opening closer to 1921, the caveat being the original building served only as a restaurant not a luxury hotel.

Joshua Paine finished the exterior of his new business in November 1921, and a grand opening was set for the following summer. It was no irony that he chose property near where the Pilgrims had first landed, as he was a direct descendant of theirs. In August 1922, the Provincetown Inn opened next to

A postcard of Provincetown Inn. *Courtesy of the Boston Public Library.*

the relatively new West End Breakwater, which had been completed in 1911. The restaurant served lunch, dinner and tea, focusing on its fish, chicken and lobster. There were special "supper dances" and music on Mondays, Wednesdays and Fridays. It is unknown just how successful the restaurant chapter of the property was. After only a few seasons of serving strictly as a restaurant, the property went in an entirely new direction.

In April 1928, the restaurant became a hotel, as an addition with twenty-eight rooms, each with a private bath, was constructed. During that first season, it focused on holding company banquets and meetings along with its "famous shore dinners." The following September, the present-day Province Lands Road was finished, allowing automobiles greater access to the beaches and the new hotel as well. By 1930, the hotel had expanded to forty rooms with forty private baths, and it still promoted its dining from 12:00 p.m. to 9:00 p.m. After the sudden death of its owner Joshua Paine in December 1932, there was a fear that this was the end of the Provincetown Inn. In June 1933, the hotel was bought at auction by expert hotel man Charles Kokerda. At the time of its much-ballyhooed reopening, it had fifty rooms and had already garnered a reputation for urban luxury and comfort. Despite grand plans, Kokerda's hotel was foreclosed on in 1935 and sold to Chester Peck. From there, things only got bigger and better for the hotel.

In 1936, new cottages were added to the property. To maximize the room the property had at the time, a large section of marshland was filled in during December 1936 to build employee living quarters. Fourteen additional rooms were built in the winter of 1938–39. Provincetown Inn was a must-stop for those who were vacationing on the Outer Cape, and rooms were in great demand. However, the outbreak of World War II put plans on hold. During the war years, the property was taken over by the navy and was used as a coast guard training station. Coming out of the war, Peck decided to expand the hotel once again.

Peck added a new building to house the Breakwater Room Lounge and Nightclub, and it had a maximum capacity of more than 250 people. It had a big debut in June 1946 with Ernie Bell and his orchestra. The inn also had a new gift shop and a new section of rooms on its second floor referred to as the "Pine and Perry Rooms." The Breakwater Room was short-lived though, as it became eight two-bedroom suites in 1950, when the demand for rooms outweighed the desire for a nightclub. The On-the-Shore Cocktail Lounge was added in the early 1950s as a replacement, and it came complete with a television. As the demand increased, and with parking at a premium in the relatively cramped Provincetown, dune sand was used to create four new acres of land along the side and front of the western wing of the hotel in February 1957. The inn's now-famous Olympic-sized swimming pool in the shape of a Pilgrim hat was also constructed in 1957. In 1958, Peck built a spacious motel that surrounded the perimeter of the parking lot. This added thirty-two rooms to the property. Chester Peck had transformed the property from a small inn to a hugely popular summer resort during his tenure.

During the late 1960s, the Provincetown Inn became a year-round establishment, with a sauna and six-lane bowling alley added to the preexisting amenities, including the barbershop, salon, scooter rental facility and three separate dining rooms. Also during this time, perhaps the resort's most beloved feature came to be; historic murals of Provincetown were painted with painstaking detail by local artist Don Aikens, beginning in 1966. These murals feature scenes of bygone Provincetown, and to this day, they attract those who don't even stay at the hotel.

After successfully creating an icon at the tip of the Cape Chester, Peck sold the inn for $1.85 million ($11.58 million in 2021) and retired in 1972. When Brooke Evans bought the inn in 1977, he remained dedicated to the standards Peck created. It became a place for high-class entertainment, like Grace Jones and Phyllis Diller, as well as a training headquarters for middleweight champion boxer "Marvelous" Marvin Hagler. In 1997, the inn took its current form when the structure that enclosed the pool was removed, a bar and grill was added and a large lawn area was planted.

Today, the 104-room resort is still in the Evans family, as Brooke's son Evan runs it. The resort remains dedicated to its high standards in lodging and dining. The views of the harbor and West End Breakwater are only amplified by the luxury accommodations inside the resort's walls. An icon of Provincetown, this inn has come a long way since Joshua Paine's first vision in the days just after World War I, and it shows no signs of slowing down.

RED HORSE INN

ADDRESS: 28 FALMOUTH HEIGHTS ROAD, FALMOUTH
YEARS ACTIVE: 1933–PRESENT

Nestled in Falmouth Heights, the Red Horse Inn has carved out a reputation for being a classy boutique inn on Cape Cod. It has well over half a century of its own history, providing generations of visitors with a sweet, simple and relaxing backdrop to their Cape vacations. However, the history of the property at 28 Falmouth Heights Road goes back even further.

In 1933, just as the Great Depression was taking hold of thc country, a ncw eating establishment was opening up in the then-quiet town of Falmouth. It was simply known as the Bellows, and its owner made it one of the first landmark restaurants on Cape Cod.

Thekla Hedlund had come to Cape Cod from Long Island during the Roaring Twenties. She operated the Lustre Tea Room on Main Street in Centerville for five successful years before deciding to try her luck with another tearoom in Falmouth. Her new venture soon outgrew anything she had previously planned for. Word spread slowly the first season. Hedlund relied on her reputation from the Lustre Tea Room and positive feedback from those customers who took a chance on her new establishment. Those who did come in for breakfast, lunch or dinner were treated to fine cuisine, including popular items like chicken pie, corn fritters and even lobster. This was no ordinary tearoom.

A seasonal spot, the Bellows set a schedule of opening in mid-June and closing in mid-September. In its second season, the Bellows's business went through the roof. Word-of-mouth recommendations had spread, making it necessary for people to telephone ahead and make reservations. The $1.50

The Red Horse Inn. *Courtesy of Christopher Setterlund.*

freshly caught lobster dinner and $0.75 dinner specials were held every night, but Sundays and holidays helped make the Bellows a certified hit. The tearoom only got bigger with an expansion in 1938. Customers then entered a large reception hall, which had white pine walls, a beamed ceiling and a large fireplace. The larger dining area was then complete with maple furniture and a spectacular view of a pine tree–lined garden.

The Bellows only grew in business and reputation into the 1940s, with Thekla and her two daughters shouldering the load. That wear and tear eventually came back to claim Hedlund. In August 1945, nearing the end of her twelfth busy season at the Bellows, Thekla suffered a cerebral hemorrhage. Her daughters immediately closed down to tend to their mother. Despite their best efforts, Thekla never again opened the Bellows. She passed away in April 1946 at the age of seventy-two.

After that, the building passed through many hands. Charles Colligan bought the Bellows from Hedlund's estate in 1946, and within a month, he sold it to New Hampshire restaurateur William Doukas. He carried on Thekla's tradition for two more years, even bringing in well-established chefs and bakers from Boston before selling the Bellows to local restaurateur John F. Sheehan in 1948.

Sheehan built a new kitchen onto the back of the Bellows while turning the old kitchen into a dining room and the old dining room into guest bedrooms. Thus, the property was transformed into a hotel and renamed the Red Horse Inn. It was then able to accommodate up to thirty-two people, with rates ranging from \$3.50 to \$4.50 (\$38.00 to \$48.84 in 2021). In advertisements from the opening, Sheehan promoted the short walk to the water, along with private entrances and private bathrooms. Although Red Horse was an inn at the time, Sheehan served guests breakfast and dinner, thanks to his chef, Edward Masterson, formerly of Chatham Bars Inn. The dining room was also opened to the public for those meals.

The Red Horse Inn's opening day was June 19, 1948, and although it was an immediate success, there were complications due to an agreement Sheehan had signed. This agreement was signed in 1946, when Sheehan had sold his previous restaurant, Town House, to Norman Yates. It stated that he would not open a competing establishment within a certain radius for five years, meaning until after 1951. There were rumblings that the new Red Horse Grille on Palmer Avenue was also going to be run by John Sheehan through his brother Joseph. A lawsuit was filed by Yates, which stretched all the way through 1949, before the judge ruled in favor of Yates. By the spring of 1951, Red Horse Grille had been sold to John's brother Edward Sheehan.

In November 1952, the Red Horse Grille was sold by Sheehan to longtime traveling salesman Raymond Duffy. It was Duffy's intention to use the property as a guest house and not a restaurant; although, the following summer, he opened a clam shack nearby called the Salt Box. Other business interests took their toll on Duffy's time, and he sold Red Horse Inn to Robert and Thomas Cashman in July 1956.

The Cashmans worked hard to make the twenty-two-room inn a landmark in Falmouth. In May 1958, they were granted permission to build a one-story, nine-unit annex on the property, with an additional two-story ten-unit annex being requested in December 1961. They brought some much-needed stability to the former Bellows, holding on to it until December 2002, when it was purchased by entrepreneurs Eleacia and Bob Fredette. They then put money into renovating all of the rooms. This began with the Red Horse Inn's "worst room," room 5, which was often referred to as the "punishment room" by the housekeeping staff. It was always the last to be rented due to its outdated motel furnishings and unflattering brown-and-orange decor. The room was renovated with new hardwood floors and a whirlpool. The Fredettes' efforts paid off, with revenue steadily increasing and the Red Horse Inn being voted one of Cape Cod's best by *Cape Cod Life Magazine* in 2005 and being a spotlight in the *Boston Globe*.

The Fredettes sold Red Horse Inn to Hamish Homan in May 2008 as a turnkey business. It finally fell into the hands of Bill and Linda Zammer in 2011; they also owned the Flying Bridge and Coonamessett Inn, both other Falmouth landmarks, at the time.

As of 2021, the twenty-two-room Red Horse Inn was still going strong after more than seventy years in service as a motel. It has achieved TripAdvisor's Certificate of Excellence and is centrally located near Falmouth's great attractions. It even keeps in touch with its restaurant beginnings with its complimentary breakfast bar called LeBarn.

SANTUIT HOUSE

ADDRESS: 804 MAIN STREET, COTUIT
YEARS ACTIVE: 1860–1925

In the twenty-first century, resort hotels are commonplace on Cape Cod. Wequassett, Chatham Bars Inn, Ocean Edge and many more dot the peninsula from end to end. In the long line of beloved and luxurious hotels on the Cape, there had to be an original—the first from which all others followed. That original was the Santuit House in Cotuit.

The story of the Santuit House goes back to the days just before the American Civil War. These were the days when the village of Cotuit was known as Cotuit Port. Braddock Coleman was a sea captain during the first half of the nineteenth century. His knowledge of the sea led to some successful ventures, including becoming a ferryman of sorts, taking passengers from Cotuit Port to Nantucket in the late 1830s. During the 1840s, Coleman and his wife, Martha, opened their home as a boardinghouse. Known as Coleman's Boarding House, the two-story French Provincial–style structure situated on a little under an acre of land was quite popular for travelers at the time. Despite this fact, Coleman sold the house in 1849.

After his retirement from the sea, Captain Coleman and Martha decided to build a new boardinghouse in 1860. Putting his previous hostelry experience to use, the new boardinghouse officially opened on April 1, 1861, with advertisements in the local newspapers to commemorate the occasion. Built in the French Provincial style, the Santuit House, as the new hotel was called, was an immediate hit, thanks to its location on the water and its impeccable furnishings and interior design. Described as having well-ventilated rooms, perfect for couples or families, the times when it was not at full capacity during its first few seasons were seen as shocking. Located nearby was a horse stable, fishing and pleasure boats and naturally pristine beaches for swimming. The Santuit House's popularity began putting Cotuit Port on the map as a desirable summer destination.

During the late 1860s, Braddock relinquished control of Santuit House to his son James Coleman. He continued the positive momentum so much that Coleman's hotel was routinely filled to capacity. His desire was to increase the size of the hotel so that he did not need to turn people away. However, James Coleman did his best to find other accommodations for those he had to turn away, including the use of some cottages owned by kindly neighbors. In the summer of 1871, he got his wish and made several improvements to the hotel, including enlarging the kitchen and the dining room to increase its capacity to seventy-five. A sloop yacht called *Edith Rose* was bought by the inn so that guests could enjoy fishing and pleasure boating from the Santuit's wharf, which was located about one hundred yards away from the hotel. Dignitaries and respected members of society from across New England, New York City and Washington, D.C., traveled to the Cape to partake in the splendid scenery and impeccable accommodations of the Santuit House. Its reputation preceded it.

In March 1873, James Coleman's father, Braddock, died at the age of sixty-nine, and then, in September, his daughter Alice died suddenly. James and his wife leased the Santuit House out to Issac Sturgis a few weeks later, and they took a leave of absence while part of Braddock's property opposite the Santuit House was sold to Asa Bearse in April 1874. Around this time, another major change took place, as Cotuit Port was shortened to Cotuit by postmaster Charles C. Bearse. James Coleman returned to the business in time for the 1875 season. At the time, rooms cost between $12 and $16 per week ($285 and $380 in 2021).

After a few more seasons in charge, in May 1877, Coleman lost Santuit House to the Barnstable Savings Bank due to bankruptcy. It remained dormant until May 1880, when it was purchased by Charles Scudder. Though it was reopened for the summer to much fanfare and was refurnished by Scudder, his tenure was short. In March 1882, Scudder sold the property to James Webb, one of the leading cranberry growers in Massachusetts at the time, for $3,000 ($77,000 in 2021). He even wrote a book, *Cape Cod Cranberries*, in 1886. Webb's first change was to keep the hotel open year round. It was the first of many big changes, including the purchase of the neighboring Captain Alpheus Adams house.

In 1888, a two-story addition was constructed at the Santuit House, and an addition was built onto the Adams cottage on the property. Webb also added a huge ballroom and enlarged the dining room to keep up with the booming business during the early 1890s. At this point, the small, charming boardinghouse that had been built by Braddock Coleman had become a juggernaut in hostelry, capable of holding 230 in its dining room and laying claim to seventy rooms, which could house 150 guests. People came to the Santuit House from all across the country to enjoy croquet and tennis, in addition to Captain Nelson Nickerson's fresh oysters and little neck clams on Santuit's wharf.

In December 1896, James Webb's wife, Abbie, died suddenly in the midst of another expansion, leaving Webb and his daughter Anna Bodfish in charge of the busy hotel. As the twentieth century began, Santuit House was seen as one of the finest luxury hotels in the region; it was firmly entrenched in Cape Cod society, despite newer resorts beginning to spring up. It was routinely filled to capacity in the years leading up to—and during—World War I. James Webb and his daughter Anna were consistently involved in local hotel business meetings, while also tending to their large array of cranberry bogs in Carver, Massachusetts.

On September 28, 1918, James Webb died at the age of eighty-four, leaving his daughter Anna to run the Santuit House as well as the family cranberry bogs. In April 1920, while on a visit to Malden, Massachusetts, to look for employees for the summer months, Anna died suddenly at the age of sixty-one, leaving the business in turmoil. Anna's daughter Abbie was left in charge, returning home from Wheaton College to assume the helm of the iconic Santuit House. The property saw a downturn after Anna's death, and it was opened intermittently, even remaining closed for the entire summer of 1924. It was then purchased by John Linnell from Boston, ending more than forty years of the property being in the Webb family.

On September 22, 1925, a fire broke out in the kitchen of the Santuit House. When it was finally discovered by William Potter, the hotel was too far gone. Despite the efforts of the Falmouth, Hyannis and Onset Fire Departments, the historic Santuit House was a total loss. A few of the surrounding cottages, however, including the Adams house, were saved. Ironically, after the Santuit House burned to the ground, the sweeping view of the ocean, which was one of the calling cards of the hotel, was able to be enjoyed by all who passed by along Main Street.

Business in Cotuit declined for the remainder of the 1920s, though the Pines assumed the role as the main hotel in the village until it was closed in 1958. In the nearly one hundred years since the Santuit House was burned down, many modern luxury hotels have risen all over Cape Cod. The Santuit House will forever be the original—the first hotel seen as a destination and the one that put the little village of Cotuit on the map.

SEA CREST BEACH HOTEL

ADDRESS: 350 QUAKER ROAD, NORTH FALMOUTH
YEARS ACTIVE: 1948–PRESENT

Cape Cod and entertainment go hand in hand. Whether amateur or professional, music, theater or comedy, the list of talented performers who have graced the peninsula is endless. Places like the Cape Cod Coliseum, Melody Tent, Dennis Playhouse and others have created a legacy that has stood the test of time. One of the original Cape Cod entertainment locales has transformed itself over time into a historic hotel that overlooks the water in North Falmouth.

It began in 1928, when well-known Woods Hole summer resident Charles Crane Leatherbee used his connections to draw in one of the most respected acting groups in the country to perform at the Elizabeth Theatre on Main Street in Falmouth. The group, known as the University Players, included burgeoning talents from Harvard, Princeton, Vassar, Smith and Radcliffe. The names of some of the University Players, in time, became some of the most accomplished legends Hollywood has ever seen. They included James Stewart, Henry Fonda, Margaret Sullavan, Joshua Logan, Kent Smith and others. After the 1928 summer season, the group desired a theater of their own, rather than taking up residence in someone else's.

After their first two choices for a new theater received opposition in May 1929, a permit was issued to build a $12,000 ($183,500 in 2021) summer theater for the University Players at Old Silver Beach. The outdoor venue needed the aide of fans to bring in the sea breeze to help cool the audience; still, it did not stop crowds from flocking to the ten plays that were chosen by the group for the inaugural season in its new home. The new theater also

A postcard of the Sea Crest Hotel. *Courtesy of the Boston Public Library.*

included the Pavilion Supper Room, which was opened for dancing after the final curtain was lowered for the night. On July 1, 1929, the theater had its opening night, and the play of choice was the comedy *The Devil in the Cheese.*

The University Players thrilled crowds six nights a week during the season. Change began to come in 1931, when the group changed its name to University Players Inc. At the same time, actors such as Henry Fonda, Joshua Logan and Margaret Sullivan began receiving national recognition for their skills. Despite their successes, the group remained together, even through another name change, going from University Players to the Theatre Unit for its fifth season on the Cape in 1932. This change was due to the fact that the group no longer mandated that its actors be current college students.

With funding running out due to the Great Depression, new management took over and changed the theater's name to the Beach Theatre. After adding new faces to the group, its nightly success was hit or miss. The new owner, Charles Abbott, added a restaurant called the Den alongside the theater in 1935. The Beach Theatre's final shows came shortly before Labor Day weekend in 1936. The theater, bathhouses and restaurant were all destroyed by a fire on September 5, 1936.

Abbott planned to rebuild a larger staged theater, coupled with a restaurant and rooms to rent. His initial plans were rejected by the town, and he faced opposition from local property owners. Through persistence, Abbott was able to build his new amusement resort called Neptune's Tryst, and it was opened on July 24, 1937. This resort was nearly destroyed during the great hurricane of 1938. In 1939, Abbott enlarged his resort and renamed it the Old Silver Beach Club before leasing it to Lou Walters, the father of television legend Barbara Walters, in 1940. Walters changed the resort's name to the Latin Quarter, operating it as a nightclub for two seasons before heading off to New York City to start a Latin Quarter Nightclub there.

Abbott resumed ownership of the resort, running the property as a hotel and restaurant again, this time, changing its name to the Old Silver Beach Hotel. He operated it until 1946, when he sold it to Frank Reardon of Providence, the president of the Service Paper Company. Reardon died the following year, leaving the hotel in a state of limbo. In early 1948, the hotel was bought by the North Falmouth Investment Company; this group shelled out $110,000 ($1.19 million in 2021) for renovations, while also changing the establishment's name to the now-familiar Sea Crest Hotel. The renovated hotel had accommodations for 250 guests, a terraced dining room and dance hall, seating for 350 for entertainment and a patio coffee shop for the bathers along its eight hundred feet of private beach. There were also plans to construct a twenty-five-cottage community on the grounds.

The Sea Crest became a popular staple for vacationers on its opening. Routinely booked to capacity with guests and restaurant customers, it seemed the only thing that could keep people away was the threat of hurricanes. The property was purchased by Joseph Mohr in 1952, and he ran the hotel and restaurant for a decade before selling to Kenneth Battles and Steve Hill from Boston in 1962.

The new owners added a heated indoor pool, a health spa and a 150-unit cabana to the twenty-one-acre resort. Battles and Hill also added a very well-known partner to the ownership group, Boston Celtics head coach Arnold "Red" Auerbach, who came aboard in 1963 and lent some of his cache to the establishment. It eventually became a year-round facility in 1971. After experiencing major expansions in the 1970s and again in 1982, the Sea Crest topped out at 264 rooms. In May 1987, Red Auerbach and his partners sold Sea Crest to the Laurel Group from Connecticut for $20.3 million ($46.7 million in 2021). The new owners spent $7 million ($16.1 million in 2021) on renovations and turned the property into a hybrid hotel and condo complex. This complex failed when the company fell into foreclosure, and the property was sold at auction. New owners came aboard and began the process of reuniting the hotel by buying condos back from individual owners.

The beachfront hotel took a big leap forward in 2010, when it was purchased by Scout Hotel and Resort Management, which is based on Nantucket. A bold and sweeping $15 million renovation project was completed in 2013, revamping each of the 264 rooms while creating Red's Restaurant and Lounge, named for its former owner. After nearly seven years, Scout sold the resort to Deleware North in July 2016 for $26.25 million.

Today, the Sea Crest is a giant, an icon among Cape Cod resorts. After more than seventy years, it continues to grow and improve, never resting on its reputation. Staring out on seven hundred feet of private beach on Cape Cod's west coast, enjoying poolside drinks, partaking in yoga or pilates, windsurfing lessons, golf and more, Sea Crest took its roots in up-and-coming Hollywood stars and created a resort straight out of a feature film.

TERRACE GABLES

ADDRESS: GRAND AVENUE, FALMOUTH
YEARS ACTIVE: 1892–1971

The seaside village of Falmouth Heights has seen more than its share of iconic establishments. From Brothers Four, to the Casino Bar and others, it has been home to restaurants, bars, nightlife and hotels throughout its existence. Perhaps the biggest name to rise to prominence in the Heights was a grandiose hotel that overlooked the bluffs known as Terrace Gables. It was considered by many to be the king of Falmouth hotels.

The evolution of Falmouth Heights from an unknown spot to a prime summer resort began shortly after the Civil War ended. In the early 1870s, the area that became the Heights was known simply as Great Hill. It was purchased by a group of Worcester men who formed a company known as the Falmouth Heights Land and Wharf Company. The first summer colony at Falmouth Heights consisted primarily of visitors from Worcester. By the end of the 1870s, Charles Draper purchased a few lots along what became Grand Avenue. He built a private home there at first; however, after expanding it somewhat, Draper allowed a few guests to stay there by 1880. The home evolved into a boardinghouse that gained the name Draper Cottage. The success of the property as a boardinghouse led to Draper expand it again in 1892. This time, the cottage was renamed Terrace Gables.

The new resort hotel in Falmouth Heights was an immediate hit, attracting the highest class of clientele. The amenities at Terrace Gables matched what was expected by such distinguished guests, and the pristine beach outside filled each room with sea breeze. During its second season, the hotel received attention for a different reason when an eighty-year old

Terrace Gables. *Courtesy of the Falmouth Public Library.*

woman fell to her death from one of the second-floor verandas. In a sad bit of irony, the woman's husband had died the same way several years earlier at a resort in New Hampshire. Just as Terrace Gables was entering a seemingly quiet—albeit highly successful—period, another tragedy struck. On Christmas Eve in 1895, while on a quail hunting trip in Pasadena, Florida, the hotel's owner Charles Draper was accidentally shot and killed. The fledgling business was left to his son Webster.

Despite the loss of his father, Webster and the Terrace Gables soldiered on. As the twentieth century dawned, it was already considered the prime resort in Falmouth Heights. The seasonal establishment was the first to open and last to close, and it was routinely filled to capacity. In fact, Terrace Gables was so routinely filled that Webster Draper had the hotel enlarged in 1902. It was enlarged again in early 1903, and this second expansion included a large industrial kitchen. Draper also opened a smaller hotel in Falmouth around this time called the Village Inn; it was used occasionally for overflow from Terrace Gables. Electric lights were finally added to the hotel in 1910, allowing greater visibility of the in-house orchestra, which played for guests either during dinner or as part of gala balls.

Webster Draper did not rest on his laurels, despite Terrace Gables being firmly entrenched as the place to stay in Falmouth Heights and as one of the top locations in all of southeastern Massachusetts. In 1911, he added the Fern Room to his hotel; it was a small à la carte restaurant that catered to guests and passersby as well. It got a quick shot in the arm when routine guest and mayor of Boston John Fitzgerald, the grandfather of future president John F. Kennedy, ate there during Memorial Day weekend in 1911. Draper's reach in Falmouth expanded exponentially in October 1912, when he purchased one of his chief competitors in town, the Menauhant Hotel. Much like his Village Inn, Draper used his new purchase for overflow from Terrace Gables, rather than enlarging his hotel.

By 1914, every room at Terrace Gables had a bath and a telephone. The hotel had become one of the most popular in all of New England, enjoying a record-breaking season in 1914, during which it had to turn away more than 150 visitors on Labor Day weekend. Unfortunately, it was not all good news for Draper. On June 17, 1918, his Menauhant Hotel was completely destroyed by fire. Draper cut his losses and decided not to rebuild. The site was used as a cottage for Clarence Fisher a few years later.

Terrace Gables continued to bring in crowds throughout the 1920s via rail and automobile. By this time, its reputation did most of the leg work, drawing guests from all over. After purchasing another smaller hotel, the Woodland, in 1922, as an annex for Terrace Gables, Webster Draper finally had to carry out extensive renovations and expansions on his hotel to accommodate its ever-growing popularity in 1928. Gone was the red wooden finish of the exterior, and it was replaced with a cream-colored stucco. It was hailed as a "new" Terrace Gables, and it was even featured in the New York travel magazine the *Nomad*.

Terrace Gables had experienced more than three decades of steady growth and stability when it reigned as the king of Falmouth Heights; however, it was thrown into disarray in 1932. On August 17, 1932, owner Webster Draper died in his sleep of a heart attack at the age of fifty-eight. Despite having been ill from recent previous heart attacks, Draper refused to rest, which contributed to his untimely demise. His beloved hotel continued on and was run by Draper's wife, Carrie.

Carrie continued her late husband's expansion of the hotel by purchasing the Cottage Club across the street in 1935 and rechristening it the Gables Casino. Although it was initially a success, it did not last, and the financial problems it caused forced it to be sold less than two years later. It eventually became the Casino Bar. Wareham Savings Bank foreclosed on Carrie Draper, and Terrace Gables was put up for sale at auction in April 1936. It was purchased by William James of Scituate, a longtime friend of the Drapers, for $123,000 ($2.3 million in 2021); he kept the iconic 125-room property virtually unchanged.

James ran Terrace Gables until his sudden death in 1947, when it was taken over by his son-in-law Adolph Kirk and Arthur Warren Smith. They, in turn, sold it to a pair from Boston, Michael Ames and Andrew St. Thomas, in January 1952. The new owners poured money into renovating the nearly sixty-year-old hotel, including the construction of a new entrance at the corner of Grand and Quinapoxet Avenues, which led to the renamed Terrace Room Dining Hall. Each of the seventy rooms in the hotel—and the property's 130 other rooms—were repainted and repaired in anticipation of a grand reopening in June 1952.

Though the hotel remained a success, times were changing—as was the clientele. The middle-aged and older high-society folks who frequented Terrace Gables began to pass away, and the evolution of automobiles and highways made long stays in one hotel less popular. The king of Falmouth Heights tried to change with the times as well. The changes in the 1950s and early 1960s included closing in the porches to create more room in 1954; turning the reading room into a coffee shop in 1960; opening a cocktail lounge called Club 46; and, in 1962, removing the first-floor guest rooms and merging Club 46 and the coffee shop to make one large "frolic room."

The crowds got younger, and the property was a success again. However, Terrace Gables had lost its identity as a resort hotel. In 1971, a final change in management spelled the end for the former iconic establishment known as Terrace Gables. Its new owners Cape Resort Hotels Inc. took the initiative and continued on the track the former king of Falmouth Heights was on. With very little changes needed, Terrace Gables was rechristened Brothers Four, the "largest entertainment complex on Cape Cod," and it created an entirely new and different legacy as one of the most well-known nightspots the Cape had ever seen.

Falmouth Heights went from a summer resort during the dawn of Cape Cod to the middle of the Golden Age of Cape Cod nightlife all under one roof. Today, the property, which once housed Terrace Gables and, later, Brothers Four, is now home to the Terrace Gables Condominiums.

WEQUASSETT RESORT & GOLF CLUB

ADDRESS: 2173 ROUTE 28, HARWICH
YEARS ACTIVE: 1925–PRESENT

When one thinks of a five-star hotel, the mind can drift to far-away locations, like the Caribbean, Hawaii and Europe. Finding a resort hotel that reaches the illustrious five-star rating from *Forbes* is difficult, as there were only 210 in the world as of 2020. In the United States, they can be found in Beverly Hills, Las Vegas, New York City and on Cape Cod, in Harwich.

Harwich is the home of Wequassett Resort and Golf Club. It is a slice of paradise on the eastern coast of Cape Cod, and it became the Cape's only five-star resort in 2016. Situated on twenty-seven acres, it boasts a four-star restaurant called Twenty-Eight Atlantic, luxurious suites overlooking Pleasant Bay, beautifully landscaped gardens and one of the most spectacular outdoor bars you can find.

The story of Wequassett as a place of lodging goes back nearly a century, with the land itself having history going back much further. The name of the resort comes straight from the Wampanoag Native name for the land, meaning "crescent on the water." In 1665, the land was bought by William Nickerson, who had previously founded the town of Chatham. The first building on the property was erected in 1807, and later on, it was the home of local historian and genealogist Warren Sears Nickerson. For generations, the home and property were synonymous with the Nickerson family.

The seeds of the present-day Wequassett were sown when the Eben Ryder House was moved to the site from Brewster in 1907. Known affectionately as "Square Top," the white clapboard home dates back to the late eighteenth century, when it belonged to Captain Eben Ryder, who was lost at sea in 1803. It was during this time, at the turn of the twentieth century, that the

"Square Top" at Wequassett Resort. *Courtesy of Christopher Setterlund.*

property was owned by Carroll Nickerson. In the summer of 1925, Carroll and his wife, Emogen, first opened up their home to "paying guests," with only an oilcloth sign and word of mouth as advertising. It was called the Wequassett House.

Carroll and Emogen's daughter Jeanette married Edwin Dybing in 1931. Dybing instantly became a huge help to the Nickersons' fledgling nine-room property. Despite still being relatively small, it was routinely packed with people who came from as far away as Cincinnati and Ontario, Canada, and included some very impressive names, like screen legend Bette Davis, who visited in 1939.

By 1941, Caroll Nickerson, approaching his seventieth birthday, had sold his property on Pleasant Bay to Jeanette and Edwin. The couple gambled in 1944 by expanding the property during World War II, purchasing the neighboring six-acre plot from Walter Whitehead, including the family home on Mill Hill. It paid off; after the war ended, guests came from all over Europe to stay at the ascending hotel and inn.

Wequassett got a big shot in the arm in 1959, adding music to the inn's dining when popular pianist Ken Manzer began playing there at the "Saloon," the area that became part of today's Pavilion. Edwin and Jeanette added a beach and tennis club in the early 1960s, as they kept on improving the overall experience for guests.

The property underwent a monumental change in November 1967. Dick and Dolly Burch, who had been visitors to the Saloon for a decade, persuaded Edwin and Jeanette to sell Wequassett for $850,000 ($6.65 million in 2021). This transaction meant that, for the first time since the land was bought from the local Natives in 1665, it was not in the possession of the Nickerson family. The Burches immediately got approval from the Town of Harwich to build seven new cottages to increase the capacity of the property. They also enlarged and refurnished the outdoor dining area in 1970 to accommodate dancing to Ken Manzer. Through developing a reputation as a high-class dining and entertainment experience, Wequassett remained dedicated to its lodging accommodations.

Despite a relatively loyal following, the Burches found business to be dipping until they sold the property to Fred Sateriale. After a year, Sateriale relinquished ownership to the Wequassett Holding Corporation. The property actually remained closed for the 1975 season. When it reopened to much fanfare for the 1976 season on Memorial Day weekend, it included a revamped menu and promises of well-known musical talent in the Pavilion nightclub. The new changes, combined with the inn's existing private beach, tennis, sailing and accommodations for up to 125 guests, made up the beginning of Wequassett's ascent as a premier luxury seaside resort. However, the people did not come like the new owners had hoped. The Pleasant Bay Group Inc., run by the McClennen family, purchased Wequassett in February 1977 for $1.3 million ($5.61 million in 2021).

The McClennen ownership took to creating a resurgence at Wequassett. By 1984, the resort had 103 rooms on its twenty-two acres, up from the forty-seven rooms when it was purchased in 1977. The popular outdoor eating area was revamped and became known as the Outer Bar and Grille in 2006. It took time and patience, but Wequassett turned an overall profit again in 1988. Though the McClennens actually put the resort on the market, no sale ever came. Their current managing partner Mark Novota came aboard in late 1987, and he was allowed to put his signature touch all over Wequassett. By 1994, he had ascended to managing partner and implemented his belief of "perpetual commitment to continuous improvement." Though there have been minor bumps in the road, it has basically experienced a steady climb ever since.

As of 2021, Wequassett was a full-scale luxury resort that was also welcoming to the general public. In addition to its 120 rooms for guests, restaurants like Libaytion and the Outer Bar and Grille combine great food and drink with great scenery. One can sip a drink around the fire pit and

A fire pit at Wequassett Resort. *Courtesy of Christopher Setterlund.*

then take a walk out onto the sand along Round Cove and listen to the lapping waves or catch some live entertainment. The Verandas at Twenty-Eight Atlantic sit just behind the restaurant, overlooking Round Cove, with several small fire pits dotting the patio in a slightly more intimate setting. There are 104 rooms in 22 historic buildings that are attended to by 450 to 475 staff members, though only about thirty of the employees are year-rounders. As one of only seventy-six five-star resort hotels in the United States, Wequassett has earned that honor through its attention to detail, not to mention its spectacular views, highly rated cuisine and its stability of the same ownership for more than forty years.

From Emogen Nickerson's oilcloth sign on the family home in 1925 to a sprawling iconic five-star resort, Wequassett has seen nearly a century of continuous improvement. For those who see it for the first time, it may seem like it has always been an oasis of luxury on Cape Cod. However, for those who own it now and those who did before, they all know it took a village of strong people to build the history and legacy of this Cape giant.

WIANNO CLUB

ADDRESS: 107 SEA VIEW AVENUE, OSTERVILLE
YEARS ACTIVE: 1873–PRESENT

Osterville is one of the most luxurious villages Cape Cod has to offer. It is home to the posh, gated Oyster Harbors. It was once home to the iconic East Bay Lodge. However, one spot was there before Oyster Harbors existed, and it is still there decades after East Bay Lodge was torn down. It's called the Wianno Club, and for nearly 150 years, the property on Sea View Avenue has been catering anniversaries, weddings, family reunions and so much more.

The land known today as Wianno was originally known as Cotocheset by the Wampanoag Natives when English settlers first arrived on Cape Cod in the early seventeenth century. It was and still is a smaller village within the village of Osterville, a part of Barnstable. It was then fitting that the first summer hotel in the village of Wianno was named the Cotocheset House.

The Cotocheset House was steeped in history from the beginning. In 1872, Daniel Webster's mansion on Summer Street in Boston burned down. Stone from that mansion was used to create the foundation of the Cotocheset House in February 1873. The hotel was meant to be a summer retreat surrounded by cottages and was funded by a group called the Osterville Land Company, consisting of Harvey Scudder, J.H. Chadwick, H.W. Chaplain and F.A. Crocker. It boasted a pier for boating and fishing, horseback riding, croquet and bowling alleys as part of its amenities on opening. Though it was a summer retreat, the bowling alley remained open into the winter of 1873, giving younger locals something to do. The Osterville Land Company sold the fledgling luxury hotel in 1877 to J.C. Stevens, who put the highly

The Wianno Club. *Courtesy of Christopher Setterlund.*

capable Thankful Hamblin Ames in charge. Ames was the first Osterville librarian, with the library itself starting in her dining room in 1873.

The hotel expanded slightly in 1878 to account for its increasing popularity. Mrs. Ames was seen as the glue that held together the Cotocheset. Her duties increased as new cottages, seen as odd-looking but substantial houses at the time, were erected on the grounds in 1883. The summer hotel was then the centerpiece of a pleasant but luxurious summer retreat in Wianno.

Things changed drastically on Sunday, July 17, 1887. In the early morning hours, a slow-burning fire broke out on the second floor of the Cotocheset House. It was discovered by a pair of servers, who alerted the hotel's nearly one hundred guests. Though they were all able to escape unharmed—even with some of the furniture—the hotel itself burned to the ground in two hours at a loss of $25,000 ($688,000 in 2021). Ames became even more of a local legend when she had lunch prepared from her own kitchen by noon of that day for the displaced guests.

Undaunted, in September 1887, construction began on a new hotel on the grounds. The new hotel was funded by a Boston-based stock company, one of the members being William Lloyd Garrison Jr. The new three-story Cotocheset House was completed and ready for guests before the summer began in 1888. An addition was built in 1889, which was nearly full on completion.

Cotocheset was the darling of the Wianno village throughout the 1890s into the early twentieth century. Thankful Ames oversaw the growing success of the hotel until it was ultimately sold in February 1916, and she was replaced as manager by Oscar Skinner after nearly forty years. This sale saw an even greater change for the summer retreat. What began as the Wianno Yacht Club was changed to the Wianno Club by Commodore William Dowse, with the Cotocheset Hotel becoming the main clubhouse and center of athletic and social activities in the community. Extensive changes soon followed. These changes included the purchase of land for an eighteen-hole golf course; the construction of tennis courts, a new dining room and a large ballroom; the installation of electric lighting and telephones in every room; the construction of a brick terrace with formal shrubbery leading to the beach; and the introduction of steam heat, as the property changed to a year-round facility.

The new Wianno Club opened in July 1916, after more than $100,000 ($2.4 million in 2021) were spent on renovations. It was a family club, with members bringing a limited number of friends, along with maids and chauffeurs. Initially, the Wianno Club had a membership of 150; although, during its peak summer months, the property could swell to well over 300 guests. The club continued to expand as the 1920s ended, adding another large ballroom and even dredging to create a yacht basin in nearby West Bay. The club presented concerts, banquets and charity events that gave more people the chance to experience the luxury property.

Though major hurricanes in 1938 and 1944 caused damage to the Wianno Club, including a large loss of shoreline facing the club, the property kept its popularity growing. A putting green was installed directly across the street, as was a large beach pavilion with a dining terrace. The club kept growing in popularity and size. The size of the sprawling estate became a problem in the 1970s.

In the mid-1970s, the club was losing money, as upkeep on the property was more than what membership dues were bringing in. The club was then routinely only half-full, though the surrounding cottages remained popular. In 1978, members suggested demolishing the large club and replacing it with a smaller one, like the one that had been at Oyster Harbors in the mid-1960s. In 1978 alone, the Wianno Club operated at a nearly $50,000 loss (more than $200,000 in 2021). It appeared that the historic building was destined for the bulldozer. Even being placed in the National Register of Historic Places in 1979 was no guarantee to save the building. The vote against demolition in 1978 won by a mere four votes, but Wianno

Club survived. A beautifully painted mural of old Wianno scenes, which was created by artist Nancy Newman in 1979, ran along the inside of the dining room wall, and it seemed to signify the dawning of a new chapter for the property.

In the decades since that close call, the Wianno Club has not only survived, but it has thrived. Coming so close to the brink of demolition made members and locals appreciate it all the more. Today, it is a haven for weddings, birthdays, anniversaries and more. It has also become a familial link for some, with generations of members and their families walking the same halls and staying in the same rooms. In a village noted for its luxurious style, only once place has outlasted all others, and that's the Wianno Club.

The exterior of the Popponesset Inn Restaurant. *Courtesy of Christopher Setterlund.*

A NOTE FROM THE AUTHOR

All of the facts and information in this book were gathered through countless hours of research using newspaper and magazine archives and conducting personal interviews with numerous former owners, employees and patrons of the nightclubs, bars and other establishments included. They are accurate to the best of the author's ability.

BIBLIOGRAPHY

ActivePaper Archive. "*Falmouth Enterprise*." www.origin.olivesoftware.com.

———. "Welcome to the Sturgis Library's Digital Newspaper Archive." www.digital.olivesoftware.com.

Amidon, Barbara Stone. *Lighthouse Inn History Booklet*. West Dennis, MA: Lighthouse Inn, 2018.

Boston Globe Online Archives. www3.bostonglobe.com.

Cape Codder Newspaper Archives. www.snow-library.com/records.

Carlisle, Robert D.B. *Under a Crescent Moon: The Story of the Wequassett Inn 1925–2005*. Harwich, MA: Wequassett Inn Resort and Golf Club, 2007.

Churchill, P. "Way Up Along: An Early History of the Land's End Inn." 1993. www.provincetownhistoryproject.com.

Digital Commonwealth. "Digital Commonwealth." www.digitalcommonwealth.org.

Dunlap, David W. "Building Provincetown 2020." www.buildingprovincetown2020.org.

Provincetown Advocate. "*Provincetown Advocate* Newspaper Archives." Provincetown Public Library. www.advocate.provincetown-ma.gov.

Sherman, S. "Welcome to Sam's Scrapbook." www.samsscrapbook.com.

Wianno Club. "The Start of Lifelong Memories: History of Wianno Club." www.wiannoclub.com.

Looking back toward Chatham Bars Inn from its private beach. *Courtesy of Christopher Setterlund.*

ABOUT THE AUTHOR

Photograph by Steve Drozell.

Christopher Setterlund is a twelfth-generation Cape Codder whose roots go back to the second *Mayflower* voyage. He is the author of two books, *Historic Restaurants of Cape Cod* and *Cape Cod Nights* (both from The History Press). He is also the author of three books from the In My Footsteps travel series, which features Cape Cod, Martha's Vineyard and Nantucket. In addition to these books, Setterlund has contributed work to the Cape Cod Chamber of Commerce, *Cape Cod Life* magazine, *Cape Cod* magazine, www.CapeCod.com and www.TravelChannel.com. He also produces and hosts the *In My Footsteps* podcast, which he started in November 2020. Away from writing, he has been a WITS-certified personal trainer since 2015. He enjoys running and photography, and he is a lover of traveling.